UNITYWORKS
Training Institute

Participant
Workbook

Name:_____   Date:_____

Facilitators:_____   Location:_____

UnityWorks Training Institute Participant Workbook

Randie Shevin Gottlieb, Ed.D.

ISBN-13: 978-1-942053-05-7

www.UnityWorks.org

Special thanks to my husband, Steven E. Gottlieb, M.D.
for his editorial assistance and ongoing support

Cover pre-press by Jordan Gottlieb

Copyright permissions by Heather Hudson

Clip art images taken or adapted from:
The Big Box of Art, www.Hemera.com

All websites and references listed
are correct at the time of publication.

Published by UnityWorks, LLC
Yakima, Washington, USA

INTRODUCTION

About UnityWorks

UnityWorks is a national nonprofit organization dedicated to promoting understanding of the oneness of humanity, the value of diversity, and the need for unity—with a focus on education and schools. We work with educators and community leaders to increase equity and reduce prejudice, to promote culturally responsive teaching, to close achievement and opportunity gaps, and to encourage positive multicultural change.

UnityWorks offers training, materials and support designed to build capacity at the grassroots. By creating site-based programs, and by helping to develop a critical consciousness in staff, this grassroots approach empowers the UnityWorks team from each school, college or community organization to design and implement its own blueprint for change.

About This Book

This workbook was developed for participants in the UnityWorks Diversity Training Institute. The Institute is an intensive, hands-on, 40-hour professional course designed to prepare educators with the knowledge, tools, strategies and resources needed to improve school culture and student learning, and to design and carry out a successful Diversity Action Plan.

The book may also be used for individual and group study as part of a self-guided learning experience. Most of the readings, worksheets, planning tools and other handouts are self-explanatory. A few of the items (e.g., the quizzes and daily review questions) are discussed during class, and the answers will be part of a forthcoming facilitator's manual. For permission to make copies of selected handouts, please see the title page of this book.

We hope you will find these materials useful and engaging. Our goal is to assist you to effectively address the diversity issues in your own organization, and to promote unity, equity and inclusion in our communities and schools.

Participants from a recent Training Institute in Yakima, WA, USA

TABLE OF CONTENTS

* List of readings on p. vii

* List of readings on p. vii

List of Readings

UnityWorks Links

- **Website:** www.unityworks.org
- **Bookstore:** www.unityworks.org/bookstore.html
- **Teaching Unity Book:** www.teachingunity.com
- **Newsletter:** www.unityworks.org/newsletter.html
- **Facebook:** www.facebook.com/UnityWorksFoundation
- **LinkedIn:** www.linkedin.com/company/unityworks-foundation
- **Twitter:** twitter.com/UnityWorksF

PART I

Overview
Key Concepts
Culture

UnityWorks Training Institute

For local UnityWorks Coordinators, Site Teams and Community Leaders

Course Overview

This course is designed to prepare UnityWorks site teams and other educators with the knowledge, strategies, tools and resources needed to develop and carry out a successful Diversity Action Plan.

Unity is one of the overarching needs of our time. Learning about unity should not be considered optional—an add-on to the curriculum. It is a critical part of the education of every student. It's not enough to celebrate Black History Month, Cinco de Mayo or International Women's Day. We need a new, holistic vision of ourselves as diverse human beings—so that differences are valued and all people are treated with fairness, dignity and respect.

Even with the best curriculum and instruction, we won't reach our academic learning goals without culturally responsive classrooms, and safe, inclusive schools. UnityWorks believes that hands-on training, an action plan, and a team approach within a larger network of support, are critical for fostering sustainable change.

Course Objectives

By the end of the training, participants should be able to:

1. Identify key concepts, goals, approaches and current issues
   in the field of multicultural education.

2. Define culturally responsive teaching and practice.

3. Explain the relationship between teacher expectations and student achievement.

4. Identify three or more institutional barriers to achievement.

5. Provide three or more examples of successful strategies for equity and inclusion.

6. Identify specific resources and tools that can assist with their diversity efforts.

7. Create a Diversity Action Plan designed to improve campus culture and student learning.

In addition, participants should become more aware of personal attitudes
and behaviors, and develop an increasingly multicultural perspective.

> "You must be the change you wish to see in the world." —Mahatma Gandhi

DIVERSITY BASICS
- Key concepts and vocabulary
- Dimensions of diversity
- Social justice, civil and human rights
- Elements of culture and communication style
- The value of diversity and the need for unity
- From ethnocentrism and assimilation to unity in diversity

THE REALITY OF RACE
- What is race and how many races are there?
- How do we get our skin color?
- Genetics, eugenics and the family tree
- Our stories

PREJUDICE, POWER AND PRIVILEGE
- Prejudice: causes, consequences and cures
- Racism, discrimination, and stereotypes in society today
- Disproportionate discipline and the school-to-prison pipeline
- Micro-aggressions and colorblindness
- Missing chapters, counter narratives
- U.S. historical perspectives, laws and policies
- Tribal history and culture
- Unconscious bias, intent vs. impact
- The power of language

EQUITY, EXPECTATIONS AND ACHIEVEMENT
- Achievement gap, opportunity gap, potential gap, diversity gap
- School experiences of mainstream and marginalized students
- Teacher expectations and student achievement
- Institutional barriers to equity and achievement
- Poverty, gender, religion, LGBT and ELL topics
- Equality vs. equity

MODELS OF UNITY AND ACTION
- Authentic voices, multiple perspectives, involving parents and community
- Stages of organizational development, diversity challenges and solutions
- Culturally-responsive pedagogy: curriculum, instruction and assessment
- Creating a culture of inclusion: successful models and strategies
- Multicultural assessment of our organization
- Creating a diversity action plan

MCE is not . . .

- A textbook or curriculum package
- A special enrichment program for students of color
- A multicultural day with food and festivities once a year

MCE is . . .

- Infused in everything we do
- It's in our attitudes, beliefs and behaviors
- Our policies, school culture and leadership style
- Our textbooks and lesson plans
- It's on our walls and in our minds and hearts
- For all students, subjects, and grade levels
- An attitude that permeates the entire school
- It produces multicultural people
- Raises awareness of diversity issues
- Reduces prejudice and division
- Promotes positive intergroup attitudes and behaviors
- Teaches conflict resolution and cross cultural skills
- It includes learning about one's own culture
- And learning about and from other cultures
- It recognizes the interdependence of all people
- Increases educational equity for all students
- Prepares students for a multicultural society
- Empowers students to work for social justice
- And moves us beyond tolerance and appreciation,
  to a recognition of the oneness of humanity,
  the value of diversity and the need for unity

© Randie Gottlieb, Ed.D.

Culturally Responsive Teaching (CRT)

			Test your knowledge of CRT. Circle true or false for each statement. Please answer honestly.
T	F	1	CRT is needed primarily in schools with a diverse student body.
T	F	2	In order to be fair, a good teacher should be colorblind in the classroom, and should treat all students equally, regardless of race, gender or culture.
T	F	3	Research has demonstrated that if we do not mention differences, students will usually not notice them.
T	F	4	CRT can be defined as teaching diverse learners to assimilate into and succeed in the mainstream culture.
T	F	5	CRT is most effective using a non-threatening festive approach, helping students to appreciate diverse foods, crafts, holidays and heroes.
T	F	6	Cinco de Mayo, the celebration of Mexican Independence, should be observed in schools with a large Hispanic population.
T	F	7	Each ethnic group has a dominant learning style, and educators should be familiar with these when developing their lesson plans.
T	F	8	Current textbooks have eliminated stereotypes and generally present accurate and inclusive information about women and minority groups.
T	F	9	Teachers may have lower expectations for certain groups, but this does not have a significant effect on student achievement.
T	F	10	Public schools in the United States are founded largely on white middle-class values and practices.
T	F	11	More teachers of color are required in order to effectively reach students of color.
T	F	12	In general, there is little teachers can do for language-minority students from low-income backgrounds with limited parental involvement.
T	F	14	With a critical focus on standardized testing and a multitude of required school programs, there is little time for add-ons like CRT.

Note: #13 was deliberately omitted out of
sensitivity to U.S. mainstream cultural taboos.

© Randie Gottlieb, Ed.D.

Diversity Basics

Elements of CRT?

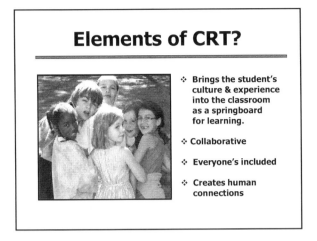

- ❖ Brings the student's culture & experience into the classroom as a springboard for learning.
- ❖ Collaborative
- ❖ Everyone's included
- ❖ Creates human connections

Triangle of Identity

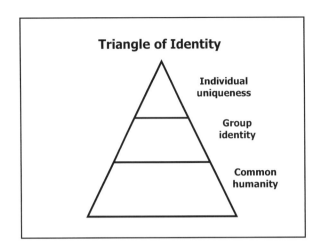

- Individual uniqueness
- Group identity
- Common humanity

Dimensions of Diversity

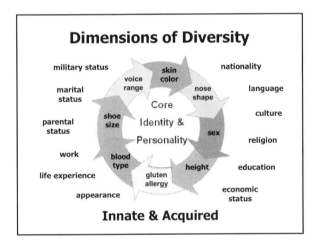

Innate & Acquired

U.S. Demographics

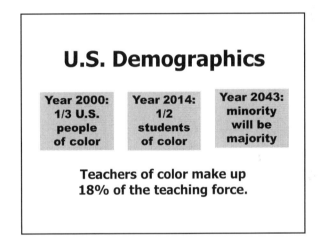

Year 2000: 1/3 U.S. people of color

Year 2014: 1/2 students of color

Year 2043: minority will be majority

Teachers of color make up 18% of the teaching force.

Continuum of Hate

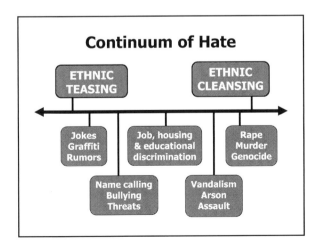

Continuum of Love

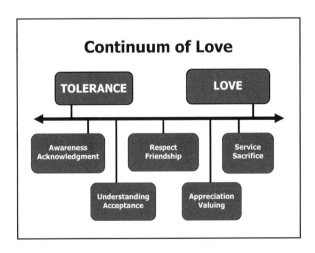

© Randie Gottlieb, Ed.D.

What's Wrong with This Picture?
An Exercise in Multiple Perspectives

© Randie Gottlieb, Ed.D. – References for #1, 3, 8 & 9 from
Rethinking Schools, Special Edition on Columbus, p. 66-7.

For each item, identify the point of view and explain why it might be problematic.

(1) A photo from a Houghton Mifflin history textbook identifies John Wesley Powell, and not the Native American next to him. The text says that Powell was the first to travel the Colorado River the entire length of the canyon.

(2) At a recent all-school assembly, 3rd and 4th grade students were asked to share their thoughts on the word of the month: *humility*. Following the presentation, teachers led the entire student body in singing Katy Perry's hit song, "Hear Me Roar," followed by the school's theme song: "[Our school] is the best, We're better than the rest…"

(3) Sample question and answer from the teacher's guide for a 5th grade textbook:
Q: "How did the invention of the cotton gin increase the need for slaves in the South?"
A: "Additional slaves were needed to work these larger fields."

(4) A high school sports team is called the "Bombers." The team logo is a mushroom cloud with the motto: "Nuke 'Em!" A school flyer with the logo adds the words: "Nuke 'em 'til they glow! Made in America. Tested in Japan."

(5) A high school honors course on World Civilizations focuses on the history of ancient Greece, Rome, Egypt, Europe, and post-Columbian North and South America.

(6) From a speech by Theodore Roosevelt, 1890s: "It is nonsense to talk about our having driven most of these Indians out of their lands. They did not own the land at all in the white sense, they merely occupied it…" (Quoted in *Racial Unity* by Richard Thomas, p. 62)

(7) From an 18th century Delaware Indian view: "The Creator…made the Earth and all that it contains for the common good of mankind; when he stocked the country that he gave them with plenty of game, it was not for the benefit of a few, but of all: Everything was given in common to the sons of men. Whatever liveth on the land, whatsoever groweth out of the earth, and all that is in the rivers and waters…was given jointly to all." (Quoted in Thomas, *Racial Unity*, p. 57)

(8) "Cortez found beautiful silver and gold treasures in the Aztec cities."
(Fourth grade text, *Oh California*, p.59)

(9) "During the 1870s and 1880s, many companies built railroads in other parts of the United States." (Fifth grade text, *America Will Be*, p. 480)

(10) A college-level text on the Renaissance describes the European reawakening in art, literature, music, poetry, philosophy, mathematics, science and architecture after the Dark Ages. There is no mention of Islam. ■

Life in the Old West

Readings about the early pioneers and settlers in the U.S.,
the discovery of gold in California, and the risks of travel across the country

From Houghton Mifflin's "Grade 5 Performance Task 2," p. 75-80

Some Risks Mentioned in the Text

- Being alone in a new land
- Being injured while searching for gold
- Getting lost in the wilderness
- Scorching deserts, steep mountains, wildfires and storms

Manifest Destiny Defined

"American settlers were destined…to expand across the land now known
as the United States until they controlled it from coast to coast."
"This idea caused problems between the U.S. and Mexico."

Some Quotes from the Text

"Not many people had attempted the journey over land to the West Coast before."
"They hoped to begin a new life in the vast wilderness of North America's Far West."
"All kinds of people were needed to settle the rugged lands of the West."
"They were drawn by the promise of free land."

Your Thoughts?

© Randie Gottlieb, Ed.D.

Multiple Perspectives in Colonial America

At the Treaty of Lancaster, in Pennsylvania, anno 1744, between the Government of Virginia and the Six Nations...the Commissioners from Virginia acquainted the Indians by a Speech, that there was at Williamsburg a College with a Fund for Educating Indian youth; and that if the Six Nations would send down half a dozen of their young Lads to that College, the Government would take care that they be well provided for, and instructed in all the Learning of the White People.

The Indians' spokesman replied:

"We know that you highly esteem the kind of Learning taught in those Colleges, and that the Maintenance of our Young Men while with you, would be very expensive to you. We are convinced, therefore, that you mean to do us Good by your Proposal; and, we thank you heartily."

"But you, who are wise, must know that different Nations have different Conceptions of things; and you will therefore not take it amiss, if our ideas of this kind of Education happened not to be the same with yours. We have had some Experience of it; Several of our young People were formerly brought up at the Colleges of the Northern Provinces; they were instructed in all your Sciences; but when they came back to us, they were bad runners, ignorant of every means of living in the Woods, unable to bear either Cold or Hunger, knew neither how to build a Cabin, take a Deer, or kill an Enemy, spoke our Language imperfectly, were therefore neither fit for Hunters, Warriors, nor Counsellors; they were totally good for nothing."

"We are however not the less oblig'd by your kind Offer, tho' we decline accepting it; and, to show our grateful Sense of it, if the Gentleman of Virginia will send us a Dozen of their Sons, we will take Care of their Education, instruct them in all we know, and make Men of them."

From International Development Review (Focus), 1974/2, p. 34. Excerpted from a pamphlet published in 1784 by Benjamin Franklin, "Remarks concerning the savages of North America."

Test Your Cultural IQ

			Circle T or F to indicate True or False for each statement.
T	F	1	Culture and race are essentially the same thing.
T	F	2	Culture consists primarily of language, music, art, dance, food and clothing.
T	F	3	Specific cultural traits tend to have a genetic base.
T	F	4	Cultures are fairly well-defined, without much overlap between them.
T	F	5	Despite their differences, most cultures show respect in the same ways.
T	F	6	You can usually identify someone's culture based on the way they look.
T	F	7	In face-to-face conversations, spoken language carries most of the meaning.
T	F	8	When people speak another language in front of me, they are probably talking about me or hiding something.
T	F	9	Language differences and translation errors are the primary cause of cross-cultural misunderstandings.
T	F	10	People are often unaware of the basic rules of their own culture.

© Randie Gottlieb, Ed.D.

Culture Basics

What Is Culture?

Patterns of thinking, feeling & doing
that a group of people have developed over years of living together

Culture includes:
- Values & attitudes
- Beliefs & behaviors
- Language
- Communication style
- Gender roles
- Child rearing practices
- Holiday traditions
- Religious beliefs...

Surface Culture

Like the branches of a tree, some elements of culture are visible to the eye.

Art	Beliefs
Music	Behaviors
Dance	Values
Food	Attitudes
Clothing	Traditions

Deep Culture

Other elements are like roots, below the surface and invisible.

Some Elements of Culture

- World view
- Notions of time & space
- Taboos, myths, superstitions
- Patterns of thought & language
- Non-verbal communication
- Values, beliefs & attitudes
- Social patterns & gender roles
- Organizational structures
- History & traditions
- Tools & technology

Mainstream Culture

Refers to the dominant cultural patterns and standards in U.S. society, provided largely by white European Americans.

The Color of Words by Phillip Herbst

Why Learn About Culture?

- To recognize ourselves as cultural beings.
- To understand the influence of culture on perception, communication & behavior.
- To relate productively to co-workers.
- To be respectful of the people we serve.
- To create inclusive classrooms.
- To prepare students for a MC world.

Sample Legislation

WA State recently passed HB 1541, mandating the development of "cultural competence training" for all school personnel. Application of this knowledge will be among the criteria for evaluating teacher and principal performance.

Some Elements of Culture

CULTURE:

SURFACE CULTURE:

DEEP CULTURE:

World View

- Meaning of life and death
- Religious and scientific beliefs
- Taboos, myths, superstitions
- Notions of time and space
- Past, present or future orientation

Patterns of Thought and Language

- Linear or other modes of thinking
- Native language
- Communication style
- Non-verbal communication
- Perceptions, symbols

Values and Attitudes

- Individual vs. group
- Material vs. spiritual
- Competition vs. cooperation
- Work vs. leisure
- Effort vs. fate
- Moral code, right and wrong
- Conception of justice
- Definition of success

Social Patterns

- Who has power, authority? Who doesn't?
- Social hierarchy, class and caste roles
- Level of formality
- Family, age and gender roles
- Approaches to decision-making
- Proper greetings and leave takings
- Courtship and marriage customs
- Child rearing practices
- Rules for dressing, speaking, eating

Organizational Structures

- Educational, legal, political, medical
- Economic, agricultural, religious
- Arrangement of physical space

Tools and Technology

- Role and importance of technology
- Major tools of the society

History and Traditions

- Art, architecture, music, food, dance, clothing
- Cultural holidays, celebrations, rituals

© Randie Gottlieb, Ed.D.

Notes: _____

_____

_____

_____

_____

_____

_____

_____

_____

_____

_____

_____

_____

_____

_____

_____

_____

_____

_____

_____

_____

_____

_____

_____

_____

Readings
on Culture

UnityWorks Training Institute

-1- **Looking Beyond Behavior** Diverse cultural responses to underlying universal needs	**-2-** **Normative Communication Styles & Values** Invisible patterns that can interfere with understanding	**-3-** **Values Americans Live By** A comparison of U.S. mainstream and other cultural values	**-4-** **American Indian Culture & Learning Styles** Comparing traditional learning styles with mainstream classrooms
-5- **Ten Myths that Prevent Collaboration Across Cultures** PART 1 Myths #1-5	**-6-** **Ten Myths that Prevent Collaboration Across Cultures** PART 2 Myths #6-10	**-7-** **Learning Styles, Race and Culture** Are there race-specific learning styles and cultural signatures?	**-8-** **Towards Cross-Cultural Competence** Adopting a humble posture of learning

① Looking Beyond Behavior

Men and women everywhere are impelled to satisfy certain basic needs for survival and a sense of well-being. To meet these needs people have banded together in groups and developed methods for needs gratification; i.e., culture.

Predictably, these methods often vary considerably between groups. For example, an Eskimo may fill his need to show concern and love to an elder by helping to hang him when the old man chooses to die; an American may show the same sentiment by striving to prolong the life of an incurably ill and suffering patient.

In both cases, the need to demonstrate love and concern is the same, that is to say, universal, but the specific behaviors to meet that need are quite different.

When we observe behavioral patterns without considering the question, "What universal need is being met here?" we may often feel confused or even frightened by the behavior because it does not fit into our own cultural program of what is considered to be appropriate in a given situation.

Another example of a universal need is the need to eat….Southeast Asian refugees in this country have often met with cultural resistance in their attempts to feed themselves: animal lovers were outraged to hear the refugees' plans for the domestic animals and pigeons they were trapping in a city park. In some places around the world, dogs are eaten only on special occasions, while in others they taste good all year long.

In the U.S., most people eat domesticated bovines (cattle) on a daily basis, but reject the ingestion of domesticated canines (dogs) even on the most festive occasions. Hindus, of course, eat neither. In each of these examples, the universal need to eat is addressed according to a cultural prescription.

When we observe how a given behavior fits into the larger cultural context and discover how that particular behavior enables the stranger to satisfy a need that you, too, can identify with, then the behavior makes sense. With this understanding, we can be more accepting of our differences and more aware of our commonalties.■

Excerpted from TAB Magazine, used with permission

(2) Normative Communication Styles and Values

The purpose of the Normative Communication Styles and Values chart is to identify arenas of difference between ethnic groups that can destroy trust and respect when the differences are unknown to one or both parties in a communication. These unknown or invisible differences in communication style and values also create difficulties because they may be presumed to be individual personality or ethical issues.

To use an example from another field, persons with disabilities often find that they are left out of conversations, not given eye contact, and subtly avoided or excluded in other ways at a personal level. This avoidance may be invisible to all but the persons with disabilities. Children are taught, at an early age, not to stare at people who are different. They are taught not to ask persons with disabilities "embarrassing" questions. In short, children are taught that it is not socially safe to interact with persons with disabilities—or anyone who is very different from them. One result of such training may be for adults to unintentionally avoid persons with disabilities, as well as persons who are different from them in other ways. As children we were not sure why we were discouraged from interacting; as adults we are often not even aware how and when we avoid interaction with others.

One cannot know an *individual's* **communication style or values based on** *group* **affiliation.** Individuals may vary from group norms because of bicultural skills, adaptation to the mainstream culture, assimilation, variations in heritage, amount of exposure to cultural norms, living abroad, or other reasons. Persons may *not* have the heritage and/or cultural affiliation they "appear" to have. Even if they do, they may vary from the group norms on some values or communication behaviors.

If individuals can vary so much from how they "appear," how can one use a summary of patterns? Even though individuals vary from group norms, research has shown that normative patterns do exist for each ethnic group.

One purpose of the summary of patterns is to help those who are ethnically "European or Anglo American" to understand that they do, in fact, have an ethnic pattern that is usually invisible to them. European Americans are not just "Heinz 57" or just "Americans," although these are common responses when European Americans are asked to state their cultural affiliation. When applied to themselves, culture is often a fuzzy concept. European Americans focus more on the present and the future, rather than trying to understand how their views–handed on from others– fit within the world community. This too is an ethnic or cultural value.

How can we adapt effectively if we cannot see how our views fit within the larger world community? European Americans do have a specific ethnic experience, a point of view, and a set of biases about what "normal" should be. That view about normalcy affects how they treat others in powerful—and invisible—ways.

Invisible biases need to become visible, and be seen in relationship to other communication styles and values. Research on intercultural communication suggests that this is a vital early step in handling discrimination….Each of us has biases; we gain our biases naturally as we are socialized within any culture or ethnic group. ➡

Adapted from Elliott, C. E. *Cross-Cultural Communication Styles,* www.awesomelibrary.org
This study was funded in part by the U.S. Office of Minority Affairs. Used with permission.

Summary of Normative Communication Styles and Values

Communication Style	Very little	Little	Medium	Much	Very Much
Animation/emotional expression	Asian,* Native*	Hispanic*	Anglo*		African*
Gestures	Asian, Native		Anglo	Hispanic	African
Range of pitch between words	Hispanic, Native	Asian	Anglo		African
Volume of speech	Asian	Hispanic	Native	Anglo	African
Directness of questions	Native, Asian	Hispanic			African, Anglo
Directness of answers	Native, Asian	Hispanic			African, Anglo
Directness of rhetorical style, "getting to the point"	Asian	Hispanic, Native			African, Anglo
Accusations require a direct response	Native, African, Asian	Anglo		Hispanic	
Directness of eye contact	Native, Asian	Hispanic			Anglo, African
Firm, long handshaking	Native, Asian		Hispanic	African	Anglo
Touching	Native, Asian		Anglo		African, Hispanic
Concern with clock time	Native, Hispanic	African		Asian	Anglo
Hierarchical membership in group	Native, African	Anglo			Asian, Hispanic
Individualism more than lineal identity	Native	Hispanic, Asian, African			Anglo
Individualism more than collateral group identity	Asian	Hispanic, African	Native		Anglo
Awareness of unearned "white" privilege	Anglo				Native, African, Asian, Hispanic
Closeness when standing	Native, Asian	Anglo	African		Hispanic

* Asian American, African American,
Anglo or European American,
Native American, Hispanic/Latino

Chart from C. E. Elliott.
Cross-Cultural Communication Styles
Used with permission.

③ Values Americans Live By*

Most Americans would have a difficult time telling you, specifically, what the values are which Americans live by. They have never given the matter any thought. Even if they had considered this question, they would probably decide not to answer in terms of a definitive list. The reason for this is, in itself, one very American value—their belief that every individual is so unique that the same list of values could never be applied to all, or even most, of their fellow citizens…

In the end, each believes, "I personally choose which values I want to live my own life by." Despite this self-evaluation, a foreign anthropologist could produce a list of common values which would fit most Americans. The list would stand in sharp contrast to the values commonly held by the people of many other countries. Which list most closely represents your own values?

COMMON U.S. VALUES	MANY OTHER COUNTRIES
Personal control over the environment	Fate
Change	Tradition
Clock time and its control	Human time and personal interaction
Equality	Hierarchy, rank, status
Individualism and privacy	Group welfare
Work hard to succeed	Birthright inheritance
Competition	Cooperation
Future orientation	Past orientation
Action and work	Being
Informality	Formality
Directness, openness, honesty	Indirectness, ritual, saving face
Practicality, efficiency	Idealism, aesthetics, philosophy
Materialism, acquiring things	Spirituality, detachment from things

* From a pamphlet by L. Robert Kohls, who served as Executive Director of the Washington International Center. The full text is available here: www1.cmc.edu/pages/faculty/alee/extra/American_values.html. Mr. Kohls passed away in 2006, and despite an extensive search, no copyright holder could be found. It was therefore decided to include the chart, with the hope that the author would be pleased that a new generation of educators would benefit from his work.

Cultural Differences: An Asian View

The following summary of cultural differences was drafted by
a group of Vietnamese immigrants to the United States.

EAST	WEST
We live in time.	We live in space.
We are always at rest.	We are always on the move.
We are passive.	We are aggressive.
We accept the world as it is.	We try to change it according to our blueprint.
We like to contemplate.	We like to act.
We live in peace with nature.	We try to impose our will on nature.
Religion is our first love.	Technology is our passion.
We delight to think about the meaning of life.	We delight in physics.
We believe in freedom of silence.	We believe in freedom of speech.
We lapse in meditation.	We strive for articulation.
We marry first, then love.	We love first, then marry.
Our marriage is the beginning of a love affair.	Our marriage is the happy end of a romance.
Love it is an indissoluble bond.	Love is a contract.
Our love is mute.	Our love is vocal.
We try to conceal it from the world.	We delight in showing it to others.
Self-denial is a secret to our survival.	Self-assertiveness is the key to our success.
We are taught from the cradle to want less and less.	We are urged every day to want more and more.
We glorify austerity and renunciation.	We emphasize gracious living and enjoyment.
Poverty is to us a badge of spiritual elevation.	Poverty is to us a sign of degradation.
In the sunset years of life, we renounce the world and prepare for the hereafter.	We retire to enjoy the fruits of our labor.

Furuto, S. (1992). Social work practice with Asian Americans. Newbury Park, Calif.
Reprinted with permission of SAGE Publishing

④ Thoughts on American Indian Culture and Learning Styles

As with other ethnic groups, Native American cultural patterns vary from tribe to tribe. Despite this diversity, there are many shared values, beliefs and communication patterns found in traditional Native American cultures across tribal groups and geographic regions.

In many Native cultures, self-determination, silent listening and observation are considered good. Competency is tested and rewarded privately, rather than in front of a large group. This is in sharp contrast to the typical U.S. mainstream academic model.

For example, in an effort to reward student progress, one tribal school announced the names of high-achieving students during an all-school assembly, and provided their families with bumper stickers that proclaimed, "My child is an honor student at the Tribal School." As a direct result, those same students all did very poorly the following year. The public praise was embarrassing as it violated cultural taboos against individualism, ego and pride. (Ref: R. Gottlieb, EMPIRE Program)

The mainstream classroom uses a lot of words to teach children. Words are abstract. Native cultures emphasize concrete, experiential learning and non-verbal communication. Children are taught to listen and observe. As a consequence, Native students may be silent in teacher-directed, large-group activities. To the teacher, they may appear withdrawn, defiant or uninterested in learning. In small, self-directed student groups however, they often contribute frequently.

Native speakers and authors may also use a different pattern for organizing their thoughts. A Native talk or article may be analogous to a quilt with an unstated theme, where each patch illustrates one aspect of the story. One can enter the quilt at any point and continue until the whole is observed. It is not necessary, or even polite, to inform the viewer, "This is a star quilt." It is obvious. Similarly, it would be disrespectful to tell the audience, "This is my topic and my three supporting points," as it assumes they are unable to think for themselves.

In short, the mainstream academic model is linear, competitive and compartmentalized. This contrasts with the holistic, integrated, cooperative approach that is more in keeping with traditional Native American norms. A question: Why not prepare *all* students to be fluent in several modes of learning, rather than requiring them to fit into a single dominant mode? ∎

© Randie Gottlieb, Ed.D

References

The Learning Styles of Native American Students and Implications for Classroom Practice, by Price, Kallam, Love: www.se.edu/nas/files/2013/03/NAS-2009-Proceedings-M-Price.pdf

Research Summary: Communication Styles of Indian Peoples, by Heit: http://www.lpi.usra.edu/education/lpsc_wksp_2007/resources/heit_report.pdf

The Native American Culture: A Historical and Reflective Perspective, by Tsai and Alanis: www.nasponline.org/publications/cq/cq328native.aspx

American Indian Learning Styles, Univ. of Oklahoma: www.sc3ta.org/knowledgebases/ American_Indian/4_1_1_0/be-aware-of-american-indian-learning-styles.html

Ten Myths That Prevent Collaboration Across Cultures

Immigrant and other cultural groups in the U.S. have been and are forced to play a "game." The game is called "Assimilation." It means giving up your own values and adopting the values of others, as a means to "success" or economic survival. No one enjoys forced or coerced assimilation, by the Borg, the dominant culture, or anyone else. The process is not only uncomfortable, it hurts; it is a violation of another's identity and inner self.

…Assimilation is actually a false game. …The real choice is not "assimilation" or "traditional values." We know that we can learn to understand and appreciate the values, expectations, and communication styles of other traditions without giving up our own.

[But] we are conditioned from birth to *not* have cultural competence in any culture but our own; instead we are usually socialized to appreciate only the culture in which we are reared….How do we help all of our staff to gain multicultural competence so they *can* administer or provide services in a more effective manner? One way is to begin to break down the myths and lack of understanding we have regarding other cultures and our attempts to collaborate with them.

Myths

1. That simply by virtue of membership in a cultural group, a person will be able to deal with others of that population in a culturally competent way. Not true. If such persons have assimilated the values and communication styles of the Anglo culture as their own, they may be even less tolerant of traditional values or styles than Anglos. Equally important, they may not be trusted by their own communities if they have internalized Anglo values.

2. That a member of a minority community who works in a mainstream agency is able to represent his or her community. Not true. Unless they are respected leaders within their communities, they are not considered by their communities to be appropriate representatives. In order to have an effective relationship with the ethnic community, trust and respect from the elders must be gained first.

3. That a single member of the minority community can represent the whole. Not true. For example, there really is no "Hispanic community" in most cities. There are, rather, Hispanic communit*ies*. Individuals from Puerto Rico, Mexico, Spain, and Peru would not consider themselves to be from the same community. An analogy may help clarify this:

Our view is like that of residents in a remote village in Australia when the first tourist bus arrives. The villagers think that the visiting European Americans, Russians and Italians are all from the same community because they look so much alike (compared to the native Australians). The villagers do notice that the tourists speak, look, move and dress somewhat differently from each other, but those differences are trivial compared to how different the tourists as a group are from themselves. The villagers then appoint one of the tourists as the representative, for not only this group, but for all of the tourists that may someday arrive from different touring companies and countries. The analogy may sound absurd, but it is sadly accurate.

4. That an agency *should* chose a representative from a minority community to represent that community's interests. Not true. Anglo agencies should not presume to select representatives for ethnic communities. Each community already has a leadership structure. Rather, the agency's task is to identify the structure and then find a common ground for communication, working with existing leadership in the particular community.

5. That, because there are so many ethnic communities, it is not feasible, or cost-effective to have working relationships with them. Not true. Selecting a minority representative will not work, but selecting a minority *liaison* can work. The role of the liaison is not to represent a community, but rather to understand the community's leadership structure, to win the trust and respect of that leadership, and to develop a working relationship between the community and the agency. In order to do this successfully, the liaison must be multiculturally competent.

6. That the Anglo or dominant culture is <u>the</u> U.S. culture, not simply <u>a</u> culture. Not true.
...For most people reared as Anglo Americans, Anglo American assumptions and expectations are presumed, unconsciously, to be "human" assumptions and expectations. If we see someone speaking with a certain pitch of voice and gestures, we assume that the person is agitated or angry; we rarely conceive the thought that we might be misinterpreting their behavior because of our own cultural norms. ...Our culturally based assumptions and interpretations are so completely ingrained that we experience them spontaneously—and invisibly. Members of all cultures tend to internalize and become consciously unaware of their own norms. For members of a dominant group...this condition is exaggerated; they are usually surrounded by people and institutions based on their set of values. Thus that system is constantly reinforced, and they have less exposure to contrasting values and behaviors than do members of minority groups.

7. That the key differences in culture are lifestyle, language, foods, and similar visible evidence of diversity. Not true. The key differences are generally *not* the obvious ones. It is often the invisible differences in expectations, values, goals, and communication styles that cause cultural differences to be misinterpreted as violations of trust or respect.

8. That cultural competence is something we each pick up, with time, by working with persons who are different from ourselves. Not true. Cultural competence is a skill, and perhaps an ability that requires substantial effort to learn. Working with someone from a different ethnic tradition does not necessarily lead to uncovering differences in expectations, communication styles, and values....
Instead of learning these invisible differences, they develop a reliable and consistent misinterpretation, which leads to *predictability* in the relationship, not understanding.

9. That collecting information from a community can be task-based rather than relationship-based. Not True. The basis for collecting information in many non-Anglo American households is personal. That is, the accuracy of the information given to a collector of information will be related to how well that person is *known* and *trusted*, not how important the information seems to be... Whether the person collecting the data is from the U.S. Census, the local university, or any other place that might have credibility for Anglo Americans, this will not ensure credibility or cooperation in other communities.

One consequence of this difference, since Anglo American agencies are usually in charge of data collection, is that information gathered regarding communities is often inaccurate; needs of the communities are often severely underreported. The solution is not to send someone to the door that "looks" as if he or she fits in the neighborhood. The solution needs to be personal. The person answering the door needs to already know *and* trust the person collecting the information in order for the results to have strong validity. In order to do this, the agency needs to work with the existing leadership structure of the community to develop a mutually acceptable method of collecting valid information.

10. That written information is more reliable, valid, and substantial than verbal information. Again, [this is] a very deep Anglo American value that is not shared by a number of other cultures. If the person gathering the information is writing down what is said, this often reduces credibility with minority cultures. Very bad experiences have resulted from allowing someone from outside the community to write down accurate personal or household information. For accurate information to be obtained, trusted community informants...may need to collect the information without pen in hand and...in a comfortable place away from the informant's home. ■

Adapted from Elliott, C. E. (2010). *Cross-Cultural Communication Styles.*
Used with permission. www.awesomelibrary.org/multiculturaltoolkit-myths.html
This study was funded in part by the U.S. Office of Minority Affairs.

7 Learning Styles, Race and Culture

© Randie Gottlieb, Ed.D.

Don't confuse race with culture. There are no race-specific learning styles. We *can* identify general patterns or "cultural signatures" for different *cultural* groups; however, we cannot know an individual's cultural patterns based on how they "look." For example, an individual with ancestors from one part of the world may have been raised in a non-traditional family, may have assimilated into a new culture, or may not actually belong to the presumed ethnic group.

So what can teachers do? Teachers can utilize a repertoire of instructional styles and assessment methods to reach diverse students. Avoid teaching only to a student's strength; also work on improving areas of weakness.

Strategies that promote learning for all students

- Instruction based on multiple intelligences
- Hands-on experiences and manipulatives
- Complex instruction with interdependent group roles[1]
- Thematic or integrated instruction
- Competency-based instruction
- Individual and group projects
- Cooperative learning and peer teaching
- Inquiry and experiential methods
- Visual aids and demonstrations
- Classroom discussion
- Group problem solving
- Constructivist education[2]
- Learning centers for individual study
- Choice of projects, activities or learning modules
- Instruction in group consultation and problem-solving skills

1. **The goal of complex instruction** is to ensure equal access to learning, and to promote academic success for all students. Classmates must work together on group projects requiring a variety of abilities, so that students from different cultural backgrounds, social status and ability levels can each make a meaningful contribution. Students are trained to use cooperative norms and to take on specific roles (facilitator, recorder, reporter, resource manager, etc.) to manage their own groups and to ensure equal participation. Research has documented significant achievement gains in classrooms using this type of curriculum. The more students work together, the more they learn.

2. **Constructivism is based on** the belief that students learn best by constructing knowledge rather than acquiring it from teachers and textbooks alone. The student is transformed from a passive recipient of information to an active participant in the learning process by asking questions, hypothesizing, observing, experimenting, discussing, problem solving, reflecting on and applying real-world experiences. The role of the teacher is to guide students through this process, which can include posing questions such as: What do we know about this topic? What do we want to know? What have we learned? In a constructivist classroom, students work primarily in collaborative groups investigating student questions and interests, in contrast to the traditional classroom where the teacher is the authority, there is strict adherence to a fixed curriculum guided by a textbook, students work mostly alone, and learning is achieved through repetition and measured by written exams.

Cultural competence has become a topic of extensive discussion. A central question is: "How do we become competent at something that is continually changing, and how do we develop a focus that includes ourselves as having differences and biases as well?"

Perhaps maintaining an awareness of one's *lack* of competence is the goal rather than the establishment of competence. With "lack of competence" as the focus, a different view of practicing across cultures emerges. In this instance, the client is the expert and the clinician is in a position of seeking knowledge.

Learning about other cultures, becoming informed of one's own cultural baggage, and trying to be aware of when that interferes with our ability to understand another's point of view, is helpful. We must also recognize how difficult that is. Keeping this awareness in the forefront of our thoughts, makes it more likely that we will limit its impact on our work.

When working in settings where poverty or racism have had an impact, it is important to note that it isn't just the norms, traditions, and patterns of behavior that influence how members of a cultural group function. It is also the way that group is treated within the wider society.

There is a dynamic interaction between lack of opportunity and the cultural characteristics of individuals and families who are systematically oppressed.

When we work toward understanding, we are building relationships, and this is at the heart of successful cross-cultural work. This is an ongoing process, not an end point.

This understanding needs to be directed toward ourselves and not just our clients. As we question ourselves, we gradually wear away our own resistance and bias. It is not that we need to agree with our clients' practices and beliefs; we need to understand them and understand the contexts and history in which they develop.

Towards Cultural Competence

The knowledge, skills and attitudes needed to effectively serve all students and their families

- Value diversity and learn to feel comfortable with differences.
- Learn about the cultures, beliefs, histories and experiences of your students and colleagues.
- Become more aware of your own cultural norms and communication styles.
- Understand the dynamics of cross-cultural interactions.
- Develop cultural humility and form positive relationships across cultures.
- Acknowledge your own biases and strive to reduce individual prejudice.
- Understand the impact of institutional power imbalances and systemic oppression.
- Advocate for the inclusion of missing voices and the right of others to speak for themselves.
- Work to create respectful, equitable and inclusive educational programs and services.

Paper PowerPoint - Due Day 2

Your team has five minutes to prepare a "Paper PowerPoint" on one of the sections below. Use the markers and blank paper to create up to five "slides" using text and/or images to answer the questions. Tomorrow, your team will have 1-2 minutes to present your slides during the morning review.

Item	Day 1 Review Topics
A	• Define ethnocentrism, assimilation, acculturation and cultural appropriation. • What is the difference between cultural pluralism and unity in diversity?
B	• Explain "multiple perspectives" and how this relates to our current curriculum. • What are mirrors and windows, and why do students need both?
C	• Define culture. • Compare surface and deep culture and give examples of each.
D	• List some elements of communication style. • What did you notice about our guest speaker's communication style?
E	• How can cultural differences affect communication? • What can we do to improve cross-cultural communication?
F	• What is multicultural education and why is it important? • Why is diversity important?

Note: For 5 teams, combine topics D & E. For 7 teams, split topic A. For 8 teams, split topics A & B.

Notes: _____

_____

_____

_____

_____

_____

_____

_____

_____

_____

_____

_____

_____

_____

_____

_____

_____

_____

_____

_____

_____

_____

_____

PART II

Culture
U.S. History
Prejudice

Your Communication Style

For an excellent description of these and other elements of communication style:
http://open.lib.umn.edu/communication/chapter/4-2-types-of-nonverbal-communication

1. PERSONAL SPACE	Closer ⟷	Farther
2. EYE CONTACT	None ⟷	Strong
3. FACIAL EXPRESSION	Flat ⟷	Animated
4. GESTURES	Few ⟷	Lots
5. HOW DIRECT	Very ⟷	Indirect
6. TOUCH	None ⟷	Frequent
7. VOLUME	Soft ⟷	Loud
8. PITCH	Low ⟷	High
9. PACE	Slow ⟷	Fast
10. PAUSES & SILENCE	Comfortable ⟷	Not

U.S. Mainstream Values

Individual	⟷	Group
Material	⟷	Spiritual
Competition	⟷	Cooperation
Work	⟷	Leisure
Effort	⟷	Fate

Notes: _____

_____

_____

_____

Cultural Adaptation

Mainstream Kids
ENTERING SCHOOL

► Our home language and culture reinforced
► Our values, beliefs, behaviors are "normal"
► We see our images, history, heroes, holidays
► Unconscious assumption of superiority
► May develop few cross-cultural skills

Marginalized Kids
ENTERING SCHOOL

► Our home language and culture invalidated
► Our values, beliefs, behaviors are foreign
► Very existence as a people may be denied
► Must learn another culture to succeed
► Feel uncomfortable or unwelcome in school

Cultural Adaptation

People have adapted to the dominant
culture in varying degrees.

No adaptation  **Total assimilation**

While most fall somewhere along the middle,
and their behavior at work or school may reflect
the dominant patterns, their internal cultural norms
and assumptions may not have changed.

> The need to consciously adapt to unfamiliar
> patterns becomes a continual source of stress.

Accommodating Cultures

**How to balance different practices &
beliefs with the good of the group?**

"Gay" activities	Allow to opt out
Sikh daggers	Compromise
Resisters	Put on planning team
Yarmulke	Make exceptions
Won't say pledge	Give alternatives

What Can Teachers Do?

How can we make our classrooms and schools more inclusive?

- Build community & create a welcoming environment
- Incorporate students' language, culture, experience
- Teach directly about diversity, prejudice & respect
- Provide an inclusive bias-free curriculum
- Bring in diverse speakers, videos, MC literature
- Teach to diverse learning styles
- Include multiple perspectives
- Use peer teaching & cooperative learning
- Assign a study buddy or language partner
- Show kids how to succeed in school
- Teach key academic vocabulary
- Let them know you care

Just for fun . . .

Circle the last names:

1. James Collins
2. Maria Garcia Ramos
3. Lee Mun Wah

Which is Nov. 14?

1. 11/14/18
2. 18.11.14
3. 14-11-18

The best word?

1. water
2. agua
3. eau

Our HIStory and HERitage

1. Who was Paul Revere?

2. Jacques Cousteau?

3. Carl Sagan?

4. Dr. Martin Luther King, Jr.?

5. Bill Gates?

6. Mozart?

___

1. Who was Sybil Ludington?

2. Sylvia Earle?

3. Annie Jump Cannon?

4. Ella Baker?

5. Grace Murray Hopper?

6. Nannerl?

With Two Wings

by Kathy and Red Grammer

> With two wings, we can soar through the air,
> With two wings, we can go most anywhere,
> With two wings, we can sail through the sky,
> With two wings, we can fly. (repeat)

I am one wing, father and brother,
By myself all I can do is flutter.
I'm only one wing, I need the other,
For the dove of peace to fly.

I am one wing, sister and mother,
By myself all I can do is flutter.
I'm only one wing, I need the other,
For the dove of peace to fly.

CHORUS

I am one voice. I am another.
I'm half of the world. And I am the other.
When we learn to work together,
Then the dove of peace will fly.

CHORUS

Some U.S. Laws and Policies Relating to Diversity

© Randie Gottlieb, Ed.D.

DATE	ITEM	IMPACT or EFFECT
1606	First Charter of Virginia	King James of England authorizes the colonists to take all of the lands, soil, forests, rivers, ports, mines and minerals.
1619	Africans brought to Virginia	Beginning of the institution of slavery in the United States.
1664	Anti-miscegenation laws	Declared interracial marriage to be illegal. Laws remained in force in many states until 1967.
1776	Declaration of Independence	13 colonies broke from Great Britain, stating that all men are created equal, and have the right to life, liberty and the pursuit of happiness.
1778-1871	Indian Treaties	Transfer of Indian land to White settlers. Created reservations.
1787	Three-Fifths Compromise (Constitutional Convention)	Only 3/5 of a state's slave population was counted for tax purposes and representation in Congress. This reduced the power of slaveholders.
1789	U.S. Constitution	Supreme law of the land. Includes the Bill of Rights, which implicitly only protected white male landowners.
1792	1st Amendment	Protects freedom of religion and speech.
1819	Indian Civilization Fund Act	Provided funding to educate and "civilize" Native American children according to Euro-American standards, leading to the formation of many Indian boarding schools, largely run by Christian missionaries. The policy was: "Kill the Indian – save the man."
1830	Indian Removal Act	Authorized President Andrew Jackson to relocate Native American nations from their homelands to federal land west of the Mississippi River, resulting in a "trail of tears and death."
1857	Dred Scott decision	Supreme Court declares that Blacks are private property with no claim, now or ever, to freedom, rights or citizenship.
1861-1865	Civil War	War between states over slavery and secession from the union.
1862	Homestead Act	Applicants, including women, immigrants and freed slaves, were given 160 acres of land at no cost, to encourage settlement of the West by individual farmers, rather than wealthy plantation owners with slaves.
1863	Emancipation Proclamation	President Abraham Lincoln issues the order to end slavery.
1865	13th Amendment	Abolishes slavery.
1868	14th Amendment	Grants citizenship with equal protection under the law, to all born in the U.S., including former slaves—overruling the Dred Scott decision.
1870	15th Amendment	Black men, including former slaves, granted the right to vote.
1871	Ku Klux Klan Act	Anti-Klan law designed to protect Blacks from widespread racial terrorism in the South. Suppressed Klan activities until 1915.
1876-1965	Jim Crow laws	State and local laws mandating racial segregation in all public facilities (schools, buses, restrooms, hotels, pools, drinking fountains, etc.).
1882	Immigration Act	First federal immigration law; calls for a tax on immigrants and denies entry to "convicts, lunatics and idiots."
1882	Chinese Exclusion Act	Severely limits Chinese immigration to avoid a "yellow peril." Koreans and Japanese were later added to the list.
1887	Dawes Act	Authorized the U.S. to divide tribal land into allotments for individual Indians, who were then required to live separately from the tribe. The purpose was to break tribal bonds and encourage assimilation. The U.S. also dissolved tribal governments and sold off "excess" land.
1896	Plessey vs Ferguson case	Supreme Court declares that African Americans are separate but equal, and that racial segregation is legal.
1920	19th Amendment	Women granted the right to vote.
1924	Indian Citizenship Act	Grants full citizenship to Native Americans.
1924, 1929	National Origins Act	Congress restricts immigration of South and East Europeans (mainly Jews) and other "non-whites" to control "undesirable" immigration.
1934	Federal Housing Administration	The FHA was created. Its handbook endorsed redlining and housing segregation by refusing mortgage loans based on race.

DATE	ITEM	IMPACT or EFFECT
1942-1946	Japanese internment	Japanese-Americans imprisoned in War Relocation Camps in response to Japan's attack on Pearl Harbor during WWII.
1954	Brown versus Board of Education	Supreme Court makes racial segregation illegal.
1961, 1965	Affirmative Action Executive order 10925 (President John F. Kennedy) Executive order 11246 (President Lyndon Johnson)	Designed to prohibit discrimination in employment and education, and increase representation of historically excluded groups. Policies require that active measures be taken to ensure equal opportunity in hiring, promotions, salary raises, scholarships, etc. Supreme Court later rules that race can be considered as a positive factor in college admissions, but that point systems and quotas are illegal.
1963	Equal Pay Act	Prohibits wage discrimination based on gender.
1964	Civil Rights Act of 1964	Landmark legislation outlaws discrimination based on race, color, religion, ethnicity, sex or national origin.
1965	Voting Rights Act	Outlaws discriminatory voting practices, including voter eligibility based on race, color or English literacy.
1965	Immigration Act of 1965	Re-opens U.S. borders by repealing 1924 restrictions on immigration. Replaces quotas with a system of preferences based on immigrant skills and family relationships.
1967	Anti-miscegenation laws repealed	Supreme Court rules that prohibitions on interracial marriage violate the 14th amendment.
1967	Age Discrimination Act	Prohibits employment discrimination vs. those age 40 and older.
1968	Bilingual Education Act (Education Act, Title VII)	Provides funding for language minority students and opens the door for bilingual education.
1972	Education Act, Title IX	Prohibits discrimination in schools based on sex. Equity in sports.
1973	Rehabilitation Act	Prohibits discrimination based on disability.
1986	Immigration Reform and Control Act	In response to illegal immigration, the Act increases border patrols, streamlines the deportation process, and punishes employers who knowingly hire illegal immigrants.
1990	Americans with Disabilities Act	Prohibits discrimination based on physical or mental disability; requires accommodations and the removal of barriers in the workplace, restaurants, schools, buses, stores, theaters, etc.
1991	Civil Rights Act of 1991	Provides monetary damages for intentional job discrimination.
1993	Don't Ask, Don't Tell policy	Bans openly gay Americans from military service while prohibiting discrimination against those suspected to be gay. Policy was repealed in 2011, allowing gays to serve openly.
1996	Defense of Marriage Act	Defines marriage as the legal union of one man and one woman.
1998	Executive Order 13087 (President Bill Clinton)	Prohibits discrimination in the federal workplace based on sexual orientation.
2000	Executive Order 13152 (President Bill Clinton)	Prohibits discrimination based on parental status.
2001	No Child Left Behind Education Act (NCLB)	Aims at providing equal educational opportunity for all students, including poor and minority children. Mandates state standards, annual testing and accountability.
2008	Genetic Information Act	Prohibits discrimination based on genetic information.
2015	Same-sex marriage legalized	Supreme Court legalizes same-sex marriage nationwide.
2015	Every Student Succeeds Act	ESSA replaces NCLB Act of 2001, and emphasizes the importance of positive school climate, racial integration and diversity.
2016	Federal transgender guidelines	Schools receiving federal funds must allow transgender students to use bathrooms matching their gender identity.

In 2015, the WA State legislature passed SB5433 requiring the teaching of a tribal sovereignty curriculum in all schools. In response, OSPI produced "Since Time Immemorial," a K-12 curriculum available at: www.indian-ed.org. The program aligns with state and national standards, and is endorsed by all 29 federally recognized tribes in WA.

In 2019, WA State passed a law (HB1624) "strongly encouraging" schools to teach students about the Holocaust.

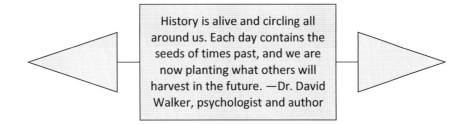

History is alive and circling all around us. Each day contains the seeds of times past, and we are now planting what others will harvest in the future. —Dr. David Walker, psychologist and author

Notes: _____

_____

_____

_____

_____

_____

_____

_____

_____

_____

_____

_____

_____

_____

_____

_____

_____

_____

_____

_____

_____

_____

Notes: _____

_____

_____

_____

_____

_____

_____

_____

_____

_____

_____

_____

_____

_____

_____

_____

_____

_____

_____

_____

_____

_____

_____

_____

_____

_____

_____

_____

The Elephant in the Room

by Terry Kettering in memory of Barbara
From Straight Talk About Death For Teenagers by Earl A. Grollman.
Adapted by Showandah Terrill and used with permission.

There's an elephant in the room.
It is large and squatting, so it is hard to get around it.
Yet we squeeze by with, "How are you" and "I'm fine."
And a thousand other forms of trivial chatter.
We talk about the weather.
We talk about work.
We talk about everything . . .
except the elephant in the room.

There's an elephant in the room.
We all know it is here.
We are thinking about the elephant as we talk together.
It is constantly on our minds.
For you see, it is a very big elephant.
It has hurt us all.
But we do not talk about the elephant in the room.

Oh, please, just say it.
Please just say . . . **prejudice**.
Please, let's just talk about the elephant in the room.
Let's admit it's here among us,
And put our heads
And our hearts
And our hands together
And figure out together how to get it out of here.

We must talk about it, for it is life and death and we . . .
are so afraid of waking it
sleeping restlessly
in the middle of the room.
We are so afraid of action,
any action, any motion . . .
waking it here
in the middle of the room.

Can I say "prejudice" to you
and not have you look away?
For if I cannot, then you are leaving me
Alone . . .
In a room . . .
With an elephant . . .

Racism, Stereotypes & Prejudice

Racism

- System of inequality based on race.

- Systematic discrimination that empowers one group and oppresses others.

- PREJUCIDCE + POWER
- Even if <u>individuals</u> from the privileged group aren't particularly powerful or overtly prejudiced.

It includes mistreatment and discrimination...

- At work and school
- At restaurants and banks
- During social interactions
- In the doctor's office

- While job hunting, voting
- Shopping, watching TV
- Renting an apartment
- Buying a home

Being privileged doesn't mean you're a bad person or your life is easy...

It means you have an unearned advantage over people without that privilege.

It means you inherited a system designed to benefit your group.

There's a difference between individual struggle, and systemic barriers based on your skin color or sex.

Some Forms of Racism

- Active racism
- Passive racism
- Internalized racism
- Institutional racism
- Systemic racism

Systemic Racism

A pattern of discrimination upheld by interlocking, co-dependent institutions: legal, political, economic, religious, medical, educational, transportation, media, government . . .

It includes racial profiling, segregation, media bias, job discrimination, polluted neighborhoods, poor schools, redlining, gerrymandering, differential treatment by teachers, doctors, police, etc.

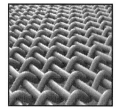

Redlining

A discriminatory practice whereby banks and insurance companies drew red outlines on a map to mark inner city black neighborhoods.

Whites were told NOT to buy there. Blacks were only shown homes in those areas. They were denied loans and were charged higher insurance rates—effectively creating a ghetto.

Racism, Stereotypes & Prejudice

Gerrymandering

50 PRECINCTS
60% BLUE
40% RED

5 DISTRICTS
5 BLUE
0 RED
BLUE WINS

5 DISTRICTS
3 RED
2 BLUE
RED WINS

Manipulating electoral district boundaries in order to favor one group over another.

Courtesy of Steven Nass, used with permission

Racism & Inherited Wealth

From slave labor, sharecropping and forced segregation, to unjust imprisonment and ongoing discrimination in voting, housing, education and employment—black families had limited resources that could be passed down to their children. During this same 400-year period, whites benefited by gaining jobs, higher incomes and home equity, passing down this inherited wealth to future generations, with a cumulative effect.

Cognitive Filter

- Our mind takes in the whole
- Filters out details that don't fit
- Selective perception
- Mental shortcut
- Affects what we perceive

When we meet new people,
our brain processes information in two ways...

ATTRIBUTES

For "us"

We see individual characteristics

CATEGORIES

For "them"

Race, age, gender... as a shortcut

Common Responses to Prejudice

Targeted Group
- Self hatred
- Turn hate out
- Play the game
- Give up

Dominant Group
- Denial
- Blame
- Anger
- Fear
- Guilt

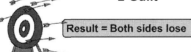

Result = Both sides lose

What Works to Reduce Prejudice?

We need to act!

- ❖ Listen & acknowledge the pain.
- ❖ Make it safe to openly discuss difficult topics.
- ❖ Teach directly about racism, sexism, ableism, etc.
- ❖ Offer positive role models, and be one yourself.
- ❖ Encourage cross-group friendships.
- ❖ Provide anti-bias curricula & instructional materials.
- ❖ Share counter narratives & missing chapters.
- ❖ Help people recognize the oneness humanity.
- ❖ Empower them to work for justice & respect for all.

12

How I Define Myself

We all have multiple and intersecting social identities.
That includes the way others see us and how we see ourselves.

1. Write your name in the center circle.
2. In each outer circle, list one identity that helps define who you are.
3. For each identity, list two or more common stereotypes,
   and decide if any of the stereotypes apply to you.
4. Then list something positive that you have gained from each one.

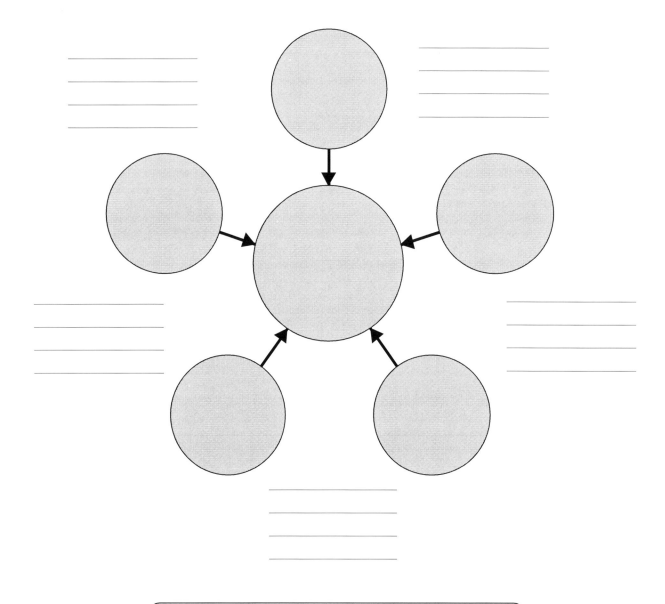

Video: "40 Strangers, 50 Questions," stepping out of the boxes
to find unity (7.5 min.), www.bravenewfilms.org/50questions

© Randie Gottlieb, Ed.D.

① OVERCOMING PREJUDICE

There is a long history of research on prejudice dating back to psychologist Gordon Allport's 1954 "contact hypothesis," which stated that positive interpersonal contact between racial and ethnic groups decreases prejudice.

Decades of investigation, including a recent meta-analysis* of 81 research studies found that direct contact experiences, along with social-cognitive training programs, were able to reduce prejudice and promote positive intergroup attitudes in children and teens. Programs designed to promote empathy and perspective taking showed the strongest effect.

"Preventing Prejudice and Improving Intergroup Attitudes" by Beelmann and Heinemann,
Journal of Applied Developmental Psychology, vol. 35:1, Jan–Feb 2014, pg 10-24

---

② Fostering Interracial Friendship

"It's easy to get discouraged about the levels of racism and prejudice in our society. We see news of black teens being gunned down by white police officers, gay children being bullied, and towns-people shouting at immigrant children to go home. We feel horrified but also helpless. Prejudice seems to be so deeply rooted in our culture that we wonder what if anything can be done to change it.

"But research shows that there is a very simple thing that helps decrease prejudice: cross-group friendships. Whether between people of different races, ethnicities or religions, cross-group friendships have been shown to break down prejudice by removing barriers of fear and doubt, and modeling new norms of behavior. Cross-group friendships may be a simple way to impact a whole community—and schools are one of the best places to start."

Jill Suttie, Psy.D. *Originally published on Greater Good, the online magazine of the Greater Good Science Center at UC Berkeley: https://greatergood.berkeley.edu. Used with permission.*

---

③ Some Ways to Encourage Cross-Group Friendships in School

1. Build an inclusive, safe, respectful classroom community.
2. Consult and decide on the classroom rules together.
3. Let students know that it's okay to notice and talk about differences respectfully.
4. Organize some getting-to-know-you activities during the first week of school.
5. Appoint a welcoming committee for new students and transfers-in.
6. Engage students from diverse groups in cooperative learning tasks.
7. Encourage peer teaching, mixed study groups, and after-school sports and clubs.
8. Assign buddies to specific students, e.g. a new ELL student or one who is shy.
9. Highlight examples of cross-group friendships using posters, stories and videos.
10. Help students to look beyond the surface and to recognize our common humanity.

---

4 To Be Hopeful in Bad Times

"To be hopeful in bad times is not just foolishly romantic. It is based on the fact that human history is a history not only of cruelty, but also compassion, sacrifice, courage, kindness. What we choose to emphasize in this complex history will determine our lives.

"If we see only the worst, it destroys our capacity to do something. If we remember those times and places—and there are so many—where people behaved magnificently, this gives us the energy to act, and at least the possibility of sending this spinning top of a world in a different direction.

"And if we do act, in however small a way, we don't have to wait for some grand utopian future. The future is an infinite succession of presents, and to live now as we think human beings should live, in defiance of all that is bad around us, is itself a marvelous victory."

Howard Zinn (1924–2010)
American historian, author, social activist
en.wikiquote.org/wiki/Howard_Zinn

---

5 Behold the Garden

"Behold a beautiful garden full of flowers…Each flower has a different charm, a peculiar beauty, its own delicious perfume and beautiful color…It is just the diversity and variety that constitutes its charm; each flower, each tree, each fruit, beside being beautiful in itself, brings out by contrast the qualities of the others, and shows to advantage the special loveliness of each and all.

"Thus should it be among the children of men! The diversity in the human family should be the cause of love and harmony, as it is in music where many different notes blend together in the making of a perfect chord. If you meet those of a different race and color from yourself…think of them as different colored roses growing in the beautiful garden of humanity, and rejoice to be among them."

'Abdu'l-Bahá (1844–1921)
Persian Holy Man
Paris Talks, p. 52

A Message from Mandela

"No one is born hating another person for the color of their skin, religion or background. Hatred and intolerance have to be learned. Even in the grimmest times, I have seen glimmers of humanity, which have reassured me that man's goodness is a flame that can never be extinguished."

Nelson Mandela (1918–2013)
First President of South Africa
On 60 Minutes, CBS, April 2006

WHAT CAN I DO ABOUT PREJUDICE?

We all belong to multiple groups. Sometimes we discriminate. At other times, we may be targets of prejudice. Below are some ideas offered by my students at Heritage University.

For dominant group members

- Challenge yourself to acknowledge privilege and how you personally benefit from it.
- Examine your own attitudes and assumptions, including an internalized sense of superiority.
- Notice how racism, sexism and other "isms" are denied, minimized, and justified.
- Avoid denial and develop sensitivity for the experience of targeted groups.
- Show genuine friendship, sincerity, informal and spontaneous association.
- Avoid a patronizing attitude; don't assume you know what's best for people of color.
- Educate yourself about discrimination: read a book, take a class, visit a museum.
- Notice the biased words and images in our magazines, movies, websites and other media.
- Watch your language, whether on social media or just joking around with friends.
- Confront injustices when you see them, whether in the market or the boardroom.
- Don't minimize differences; we are not all the same.
- Listen to and validate the hurtful stories.
- Talk with your children about racism.
- Work with other dominant group members to raise awareness.
- Become an advocate for positive multicultural change.

> **Implicit Attitude Test**
> www.tolerance.org/activity/
> test-yourself-hidden-bias

For target group members

- Be aware of the effects of internalized oppression.
- Develop a positive self identity, empowerment and self respect.
- Don't belittle or avoid contact with your own group.
- Don't compromise your integrity by becoming like the dominant group just to fit in.
- Differentiate between dominant group members and the dominant system.
- Learn to work with receptive allies from the dominant group.
- Avoid suspicion and offer a warm response to their efforts.
- Choose your battles wisely.
- Be willing to forgive.

For all of us

- Avoid denial, guilt, blame, fear and hostility.
- Instead try genuine love, true humility, tact and wisdom.
- Realize that prejudice is learned and can be unlearned.
- Make a personal commitment to change.
- See people as individuals, not stereotypes.
- Don't listen to or tell racist or sexist jokes.
- Speak out against biased remarks and other forms of discrimination.
- Work within your institutions and social groups to eliminate racism, sexism, etc.
- Make friends from other backgrounds; invite them to your home and visit theirs.
- Recognize the oneness of humanity and the value of diversity.
- Teach your children to be prejudice free.
- Join groups working for unity in your community, and advocate at the state and national levels.
- Be patient and persistent; it will take time.

© Randie Gottlieb, Ed.D.

Notes: _____

_____

_____

_____

_____

_____

_____

_____

_____

_____

_____

_____

_____

_____

_____

_____

_____

_____

_____

_____

_____

_____

Paper PowerPoint - Due Day 3

Your team has five minutes to prepare a "Paper PowerPoint" on one of the sections below. Use the markers and blank paper to create up to five "slides" using text and/or images to answer the questions. Tomorrow, your team will have 1-2 minutes to present your slides during the morning review.

Item	Day 2 Review Topics
A	• How do students from the dominant culture and those from other languages and cultures experience school differently?
B	• In U.S. history, what has been the response to diversity? Give some examples. • What is the melting pot? Is it an accurate description? Why or why not?
C	• Define these terms and give an example of each: prejudice, discrimination, stereotype, confirmation bias. • Explain the concept of privilege, and give a concrete example.
D	• Define racism and explain the difference between active, unintentional, internalized, institutional and systemic racism, with an example of each. • What is "the other tradition" with regard to race relations in the U.S.? Examples?
E	• Define microaggressions, give some examples, and explain their effects. • Explain the difference between intent and impact.
F	• Define missing chapters and counter narratives and give an example of each. • What are some other things educators can do to make schools and classrooms more equitable, welcoming and inclusive?

Note: For 5 teams, combine topics D & E. For 7 teams, split topic C. For 8 teams, split topics C & D.

Notes: _____

_____

_____

_____

_____

_____

_____

_____

_____

_____

_____

_____

_____

_____

_____

_____

_____

_____

_____

_____

_____

_____

_____

_____

_____

PART III

Reality of Race
Power of Language

# The Reality of Race

- Why do most people from Northern Europe have light skin?
- Why do many Africans have dark skin and tightly-curled hair?
- Is there such a thing as German blood?
- Are there any pure races?
- Are differences more than skin deep?
- Is there a relationship between race and intelligence?
- How can we teach children about physical differences?
- What box should I check on the census form?

How many races?

Definition of race:

Notes:

_____

_____

_____

_____

_____

_____

_____

_____

_____

_____

Racial Categories & the Law

Blacks & Whites in US Schools

> Slavery (1619-1865) – illegal to teach slaves to read or write
> Jim Crow segregation laws (1876-1965)

* 1870 – Virginia: illegal for black and white
  children to attend the same school
* 1896 – Plessey v. Ferguson: Supreme Court "separate but equal"
* 1954 – Brown v. Board of Education: outlaws segregation
  in public schools, but it continues anyway
* 1964 – Civil Rights Act outlaws segregation in all public facilities
* 1970-1990s – Violent opposition to school desegregation
  across the country (Boston, Charlotte, Denver...)
* Today – Disproportionate discipline & school-to-prison pipeline

> "New Jim Crow" - mass incarceration of Black males

1

Origins of Concept of Race
Prof. Anthony Appiah, Harvard University

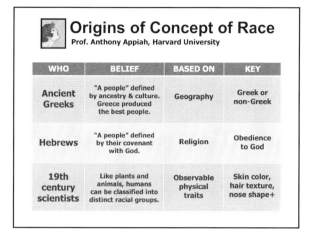

WHO	BELIEF	BASED ON	KEY
Ancient Greeks	"A people" defined by ancestry & culture. Greece produced the best people.	Geography	Greek or non-Greek
Hebrews	"A people" defined by their covenant with God.	Religion	Obedience to God
19th century scientists	Like plants and animals, humans can be classified into distinct racial groups.	Observable physical traits	Skin color, hair texture, nose shape+

One-Drop Rule

▶ Someone who looks white is considered black anyway.
▶ Due to an invisible touch (one drop) of "black blood."
▶ Arose in the 1830s North and spread throughout the nation.
▶ Upheld in court decisions and became law.
▶ Pushed many white families to the black
  side of the color line as punishment
  for associating with or defending
  blacks during Jim Crow.

onedroprule.org

U.S. Census Categories

1790 – First census (3 choices)
- Free white male
- Free white female
- Slave (counted as 3/5 person)

1890 – Added as separate races
- Chinese
- Japanese
- Mulatto (1/2 black)
- Quadroon (1/4 black)
- Octoroon (1/8 black)

U.S. Census Categories

Statistics on race are used to:
> Enforce civil rights laws,
  including the Voting Rights Act
> Monitor disparities in education
> Ensure equal access to health care
> Promote equal employment opportunities
> Allocate federal funds as provided by law
> Determine state legislative boundaries
> Measure the diversity of our nation

Race in Religion

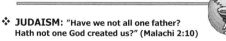

❖ JUDAISM: "Have we not all one father?
  Hath not one God created us?" (Malachi 2:10)

❖ CHRISTIANITY: "God hath made of one blood all nations
  of men for to dwell on all the face of the earth." (Acts 17:26)

❖ ISLAM: "O mankind! We created you from a single pair
  of a male and a female and made you into nations and
  tribes." (Qur'an 49.13)

❖ BAHÁ'Í: "Regard ye not one another as strangers.
  Ye are the fruits of one tree, and the leaves of one branch."
  (Tablets of Baha'u'llah, p. 163)

❖ LAKOTA: "Mitakuye oyasin" (We are all related.)

© Randie Gottlieb, Ed.D.

Readings on Race

UnityWorks Training Institute

-1- **The Place of Race** Skin color, natural selection, evolution and "pure" races	-2- **Eugenics, Race & Intelligence** Improving the human gene pool, IQ testing, ability and heredity	-3- **Problems with Concept of Race** Changing definitions of race and ethnicity, census boxes	-4- **Race: Power of an Illusion** The generational advantages of being white
-5- **I Don't See Color** The concept of colorblindness and "we're all just human"	-6- **On Being Black in America** One man's personal experience; and he's not alone	-7- **Learning About Differences** Teaching young children about skin color, race and culture	-8- **10 Things Everyone Should Know About Race***

* Item #8 is not a reading, and is included for reference only.

The Place of Race

Excerpts from "Ever Adaptive, Humans Defy Easy Stereotype Called Race" by Boyce Rensberger, Washington Post. Used with permission of the author.

You're not a racist. You know that deep down inside, all people are pretty much the same, no matter what color their skin or what shape their eyelids. But you are curious about differences among these groups that we call races. Everybody is.

Why do most people from Europe have pale skin? Why do most Africans and most Europeans--and their descendants in this country--have eyes that are shaped alike but are so different from an Asian's eyes? Or maybe you wonder why people come in so many colors and facial forms in the first place. And many people wonder whether the differences are more than skin deep.

These are honest, scientifically worthy questions. In fact, scientists have tried for centuries to answer them. After discarding many mistakes in their interpretations, today's researchers generally agree on three discoveries:

(1) There are many more differences among people than the obvious ones such as skin color and facial form. Dozens of other variations have been found that are more than skin deep.

(2) These differences have been good for the human species. If we were not so diverse, we would not be such an evolutionary success. For example, without protection of dark skin, our ancestors in Africa could not have survived the strong tropical sun. And when some of those ancestors migrated to the climate of northern Europe, where there is less sunlight, they could not have survived unless they lost most of their skin color.

(3) The third conclusion is probably the hardest to understand--races don't really exist, at least not outside our imaginations. We all use the word "race" as if it meant something specific and clear-cut. We talk and act as if blacks, whites and others belong to different groups that developed naturally long ago. But, according to most anthropologists today, that

isn't true. They say races are mostly arbitrary categories invented by people to fit a misunderstanding about how human beings evolved.

A few centuries ago, European scientists claimed that races were natural divisions of the human species. Some even argued that races represented a series of evolutionary stages, some "more advanced" than others. The old-time researchers knew of very few differences among various peoples and did not fully understand how evolution works. In fact, the concept of race was developed long before 1859, when Charles Darwin, the English naturalist, published his discoveries....

In 1735, Carl von Linne, the Swedish naturalist better known as Linnaeus, said there were four races. Over the years dozens of other classifications have been proposed, some arguing that there are as many as 31 or even 37 races.

Today, anthropologists are aware of many differences that were never noticed before and that don't correspond to racial categories. More important, the further that researchers study people worldwide, the more they realize that if they take into account all the hidden differences, they get a very different picture of what is similar or dissimilar among groups. If you consider each feature by itself, you see that a person of one race can be more like a person of another race than he or she is like someone of their own race.

Take blood for example. African blacks may be any of the four major blood types: A, B, O and AB. The same is true of European whites and of Asiatic peoples. If you're a type O, your blood is more closely related to that of any other type O person--regardless of race--than it is to a type B or type A of your own race. If you need a blood transfusion, you shouldn't care whether the donor's skin color is like yours. The same is true of organ transplants. Your closest genetic match for a donated kidney, for example, could easily be somebody of another "race."

The same race-blind relationships are true of many physical factors, from the critical to the trivial. Take ear wax, which comes in two kinds. One is wet and sticky; the other is dry and crumbly. The vast majority of Africans and Europeans have the same kind--wet and sticky. The vast majority of Asians have the dry kind.

We can also look at racial differences from another angle. Lots of people think skin color is a major factor in pigeonholing people in racial groups. Yes, it is true that most Africans and their descendants have skin that is darker than that of most Europeans and their descendants. But millions of people in India, classified by some anthropologists as members of the "Caucasoid," or "white," race, have darker skin than most Americans who call themselves black. Does their black skin mean they should be grouped with black Africans? Or does their straight hair mean they should be grouped with Europeans?

…And here's another angle to think about. If you want to classify all black Africans in one group, how do you deal with the fact that within Africa live several kinds of people with much more dramatic differences than skin color? There are the world's smallest people the Mbuti pygmies of Zaire, who average 4 foot 7 inches and whose size is very similar to that of a group in the Philippines called the Negritos. And there are the world's tallest, the Tutsi of Rwanda, who average 6-foot-1--close to the average for the very pale-skinned Scandinavian peoples. The two African groups live just a few hundred miles apart but have remain ed separate. In size, they more closely resemble other ethnic groups who live very far away.

Such differences within the usual broad racial groups have led most anthropologists to say it makes no sense to think that races are biological categories…

So how come people are different?
Biologists say most racial differences arose as a result of a process called natural selection. …In a nutshell, it means that if a mutation--a change in a person's genes--produces a useful feature, the person with that change is more likely to be healthier, live longer and, most important for evolution, have more children.

Since the change is in the genes, the children inherit it. Because the change gives each person an advantage in survival, eventually those with it will outnumber those without it.

Skin color provides an excellent example.
People whose ancestors have lived a long time in the tropics have dark skin. And the farther people lived from the equator, the lighter their skin. Even southern Europeans usually are darker than northern Europeans. In Africa, the darkest skins are near the equator, but at the north and south ends of the continent, the skins are lighter. In southern India, many people are as dark as the blackest Africans while northern Indians are about as light as southern Europeans. Whatever the skin color, it is all due to different amounts of a dark brown substance called melanin.

This north-south spectrum has evolved in response to the sun's intensity in local regions. Too much sun causes sunburn and skin cancer. Too little deprives the body of vitamin D. Without this vitamin, bones grow crooked, resulting in a disease called rickets. In the tropics, the sun is so strong that enough gets through dark skin to make all the vitamin D a person needs. When dark-skinned people first migrated out of Africa and into northern climates, they may well have suffered rickets, which also can deform the pelvis, making childbirth dangerous or impossible. But because skin color can vary slightly even within a family, lighter-skinned children would be less affected. As a result, they would probably have more children than their darker relatives. And those children would be even more likely to have lighter-skinned children of their own. After many generations, the natural effect of the combination of dark skin and low sunlight would select for people who had lost more and more of their original color. This is Darwin's natural selection at work.

Only a few external differences other than color appear to provide a survival advantage. The strongest case can be made for nose shape. People native to colder or drier climates tend to have longer, more beak-shaped noses than those living in hot and humid regions. This is because the nose's job is to warm and humidify air before it reaches the sensitive lungs. The longer the air's path to the lungs, the warmer and more humid the air.

Migration is a key player in the evolutionary drama. Geneticists know that if all members of a species stay in one breeding population, all will stay the same or change in the same ways. But if some members move away and become isolated from the rest of the species, the two groups evolve in different ways…

Although reproductive isolation is essential to produce differences, there is plenty of evidence that no group of humans has stayed isolated for more than a few thousand years. A very long separation between two groups allows their genes to become so different that the groups can no longer interbreed. The fact that all peoples can intermarry and have healthy children proves that we all remain members of the same species.

Sexual selection plays a role. Most visible differences among people have no practical advantage. For example, nobody knows why Asiatic people have that special form of upper eyelid or flatter facial profiles. The thin lips of northern Europeans and many Asians have no known advantage over the full lips of many Africans and Middle Eastern peoples. Why do white men go bald so much more often than the men of other backgrounds?

…One possible explanation is another evolutionary process that Darwin also discovered--sexual selection. This differs from natural selection, in which the environment chooses who will survive. In sexual selection, the choice is up to the prospective mate. In simple terms, ugly persons will be less likely to find mates and pass on their genes than will beautiful people. And, of course, the definition of beauty varies from culture to culture…

Our differences are trivial in a biological sense. In fact, geneticists have estimated that the variations in genetic makeup that account for racial differences occupy only about 0.01 percent of our genes.

So, were there ever pure races? Until the mid-20th century, most researchers assumed

that so-called pure races once existed. Those early thinkers had great trouble figuring out who belonged in which race and decided that was simply because migrations and inter-marriage had mixed up, or blended, the once-distinct traits. Today, most anthropologists hold that pure races never existed. They think that human beings have always been migrating and intermarrying, spreading new genes worldwide.

Genes useful in all parts of the world would spread quickly--those, for example, that might improve the immune system. Surely the fastest to spread were the genes that improved the brain. In fact, anthropologists who study the earliest human beings agree that a fully modern brain evolved long before any of today's races came into existence.

Genes useful only in some areas would tend not to become common when they were carried to other places. Dark skin, for example, is not an advantage in cold climates. Light skin is a serious disadvantage in tropical climates. So skin color genes could not flow far and persist, at least not until the age of milk fortified with vitamin D, large hats and long sleeves. The bottom line, anthropologists agree, is that science does not support the idea of races as natural units, now or in the past.

…You cannot pick just one or even a few traits and claim they define a biological category. People have tried to do this using the most visible features such as skin color and facial form, but have ignored all unseen genetic variability, which doesn't fit the visible pattern. Perhaps if humans were blind to everything but ear wax, we would say there are two races. If all that mattered was ABO blood type, we would argue that there are four races.

So What? After the many misunderstandings of the past, the great lesson of anthropology, biology and genetics is that all people are the same in the essentials, but are highly diverse in a few things. These differences have arisen not because there are fundamentally different kinds of people, but simply because we are a restless, curious, hopeful migratory species whose intelligence has allowed us to make a good living in almost every environment on Earth…∎

© Randie Gottlieb, Ed.D.

Eugenics is a pseudo-scientific social movement which aims to improve the human gene pool through selective breeding and the elimination of those with "undesirable" traits—a type of ethnic cleansing. Eugenics played a significant role in the history and culture of the United States prior to World War II.

The term was coined by Sir Francis Galton, who defined eugenics as "the self-direction of human evolution" designed "to replace Natural Selection by other processes that are more merciful." Galton's 1869 book, *Hereditary Genius*, includes a chapter entitled "The Comparative Worth of Different Races."[1]

The eugenics movement advocated the pursuit of a pure Nordic/Aryan "master race" with superior genes (white, blond-haired, blue-eyed, tall, strong, noble, talented), and the eventual elimination of those deemed unfit to reproduce (emancipated Negroes, immigrant Asian laborers, Indians, Hispanics, Southern and East Europeans, Italians, Jews, the poor, vagrants, blind, deaf, feeble-minded, drunks, disabled, orphans, the infirm, criminals and others deemed morally undesirable). At the time, many eugenicists believed that poverty, promiscuity and other social conditions were inherited traits.

They supported strict immigration and anti-miscegenation laws, compulsory sterilization, forced abortion, segregation, deportation, and in some cases euthanasia. Forced sterilization, segregation laws and marriage restrictions were enacted in twenty-seven states. Between 1907 and 1963, over 64,000 individuals were sterilized under eugenic legislation in the U.S., including over 2,000 involuntary sterilizations performed on poor Black women without their knowledge or consent. The Indian Health Service also repeatedly refused to deliver Native American babies until their mothers, while in labor, consented to be sterilized.[2]

In the early 1900s, eugenics grew into a world-wide movement led by respected American scientists and scholars from prestigious universities including Harvard, Stanford, Princeton and Yale. The movement was championed by a number of prominent thinkers including Winston Churchill, Alexander Graham Bell and Teddy Roosevelt, who wrote: "…society has no business to permit degenerates to reproduce their kind. It is really extraordinary that our people refuse to apply to human beings such elementary knowledge as every successful farmer is obliged to apply to his own stock breeding."[3]

The American Eugenics Society established "Better Babies" and "Fitter Families" contests to popularize eugenics at state agricultural fairs, where human "stock" competed for prizes in judging similar to contests for cows, pigs and produce.

By 1910, a large and dynamic network of professional organizations was engaged in national eugenics projects, including the American Breeder's Association, the Race Betterment Foundation, the Carnegie Institution for Experimental Evolution, and the Eugenics Record Office. Their work received generous funding from the Carnegie and Rockefeller Foundations, and other wealthy philanthropists.

Three International Eugenics Conferences were convened (1912, 1921 and 1932) to discuss global programs to improve human heredity, and the 1936 meeting of the International Federation of Eugenics Organizations was attended by 50 delegates from 20 countries.

The eugenics movement had a significant influence on U.S. immigration policy, contributing to passage of the Chinese Exclusion Act, the Immigration Restriction Act of 1924, and similar laws designed to stem the flood of "inferior stock" polluting the national gene pool.

Even the U.S. Supreme Court endorsed eugenics when, in its Buck v. Bell decision of 1927, Justice Oliver Wendell Holmes wrote, "It is better for all the world, if instead of waiting to execute degenerate offspring for crime, or to let them starve for their imbecility, society can prevent those who are manifestly unfit from continuing their kind…" The ruling legitimized compulsory sterilization laws around the country as a whole "for the protection and health of the state" and "to prevent our being swamped with incompetence."[4]

The U.S. eugenics movement also provided inspiration for the racist policies of Nazi Germany. During the Nuremberg trials after World War II, Nazi war criminals quoted Justice Holmes' words in their own defense. By the end of the war, however, many eugenics laws were largely abandoned, a result of their association with the genocidal atrocities of the Holocaust.

Before the war, eugenics was widely accepted in the U.S. academic community and became a popular scientific discipline. By 1928 there were 376 separate university courses enrolling over 20,000 students.[2]

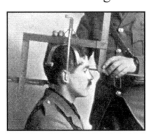

Anthropologists calculated skull volume to estimate brain size and intelligence. Doctors measured body build, studied facial features, compared muscle strength and reaction times to assess human worth. Inventors developed craniometers and other tools to measure and classify diverse ethnic groups.

Professors wrote textbooks on eugenics for teacher education programs and high school biology classes. Middle school students were assigned "values clarification exercises" where they were asked to rank people in terms of their worth to society.

In 1916, Lewis Terman, Stanford University Professor and a prominent eugenicist who helped develop the Stanford-Binet intelligence test, observed persistent racial group differences on IQ test scores. Believing these differences to be genetic, and based on the idea that a single test score could measure human potential, he recommended that standardized IQ tests be used in schools, and that children from low-performing groups (Indians, Mexicans and Negroes) "should be segregated into separate classes [and] made into efficient workers" to better serve society's needs.[5]

The process of testing and tracking soon became standard educational practice in the U.S. While rigid tracking systems that begin in kindergarten and permanently assign students to vocational, general or college prep curriculum paths have largely been dismantled today, tracking remains controversial and many schools still practice it in various forms. The U.S. Department of Education's Office for Civil Rights recently noted that "tracking perpetuates a modern system of segregation that favors White students and keeps students of color, many of them Black, from long-term equal achievement."[6]

In 1969, a very public debate on race and intelligence was ignited with the publication of an article in The Harvard Educational Review by Arthur Jensen, a psychologist at the University of California, Berkeley.

Dr. Jensen maintained that a 15-point difference in IQ scores between Blacks and Whites was largely based on fixed genetic differences.[7]

In 1994, the debate was rekindled with the publication of Charles Murray and Richard Hernstein's controversial book, *The Bell Curve: Intelligence and Class Structure in American Life*, where they argue that intelligence is immutable, primarily genetically based, and reducible to a single number which can be accurately measured by IQ tests. They conclude that Blacks score lower than Whites on such tests due to racial differences in intelligence, stating, "This difference is not the result of test bias, but reflects differences in cognitive functioning." The authors emphasize that their work has significant implications for policies on immigration, affirmative action, education, employment, crime, welfare and family planning, and they suggest that any government efforts to improve economic opportunities for the poor, especially poor Blacks, are likely to fail, because their poverty is largely the result of inherited low intelligence.[8]

 The book stirred a fierce national outcry, but were they correct? Is there a genetic difference in intelligence between Blacks and Whites? In his 1997 response, "The Bell Curve Flattened," Nicholas Lemann (former Dean of the Columbia University Graduate School of Journalism, award-winning author, and staff writer for The New Yorker) notes that subsequent research by numerous experts in the field has seriously undercut the claims of The Bell Curve. He also points out that the book is full of mistakes, sloppy reasoning, incorrect citation of sources, and outright mathematical errors.[9]

We now know that intelligence is multidimensional, that a single number cannot accurately reflect an individual's ability, that IQ can change over time, that scores have improved between generations, that "racial" differences in IQ are due to environmental factors such as socio-economic and educational inequality rather than genetics, and perhaps most importantly, that there is only one human race.

The influence of the environment on IQ scores is revealed by the Flynn effect—named for New Zealand researcher James Flynn, who observed the significant year-after-year increase in IQ scores throughout the world, most likely explained by improved childhood nutrition and better education. In the U.S. alone, scores jumped by 18 points between 1947 and 2002, making it highly unlikely that genetics could be responsible for this rapid increase.[10]

In his 2007 article, "All Brains Are the Same Color," Richard Nisbett, Professor of Psychology at the University of Michigan, states that "Hereditarians begin with the assertion that 60-80% of variation in IQ is genetically determined. However, most estimates of heritability have been based almost exclusively on studies of middle-class groups. For the poor, a group that includes a substantial proportion of minorities, heritability of IQ is very low, in the range of 10-20%…This means that for the poor, improvements in environment have great potential to bring about increases in IQ…We know that the IQ difference between Black and White 12-year-olds has dropped to 9.5 points from 15 points in the last 30 years—a period that was more favorable for Blacks in many ways than the preceding era."[11]

Regarding the assertion that brain size is correlated with intelligence and that Blacks have smaller brains than Whites, Nisbett notes that the difference in brain size between men and women is significantly greater than that between Blacks and Whites, yet on the average, men and women score about the same on IQ tests.

He also states that "about 25% of the genes in the American Black population are European, meaning that the genes of any individual can range from 100% African to mostly European. If European intelligence genes are superior, then Blacks who have relatively more European genes ought to have higher IQ's…During World War II, both Black and White American soldiers fathered children with German women. Thus some of these children had 100% European heritage and some had substantial African heritage. Tested in later childhood, the German children of the White fathers were found to have an average IQ of 97, and those of the Black fathers had an average of 96.5, a trivial difference."

Today, although discredited by modern science, misunderstandings promoted by the eugenics movement are still widespread. They can be seen in the attitudes towards immigrants from certain regions of the world, in race-based explanations for the persistent achievement gap, in the school-to-prison pipeline disproportionately affecting students of color, in stereotypical descriptions of "the culture of poverty," in reality TV shows where the weaker contestants are "voted off the island,"

and in the enduring prejudices towards those of diverse ethnic and socioeconomic groups.

In addition, there are a growing number of organizations proclaiming the notion of a superior race. Wikipedia lists over 60 pages of self-identified "White Supremacist Groups in the U.S." including the American Nazi Party, the Aryan Nation and the Ku Klux Klan. The Southern Poverty Law Center has identified 939 active hate groups in this country—a 56% increase since 2000. The Department of Justice estimates that over 250,000 hate crimes occur every year, with about half (51%) motivated by race/ethnicity—compared to 22% in 2004 and 30% in 2011.[12]

With the completion of the Human Genome Project in 2003,[13] and the realization that we share 99.9% of our DNA, isn't it time to recognize that we *are* one human family, to value our diversity, and to treat each other with justice and respect? Rather than focusing on skull measurements and racial classifications—which have caused so much harm to humanity as a whole, the science of human origins can be used to help heal those wounds. ∎

References
1. en.wikipedia.org/wiki/Francis_Galton + galton.org
2. wikipedia.org > see Eugenics + Eugenics in the United States
3. www.dnalc.org/view/11219-T-Roosevelt-letter-to-C-Davenport-about-degenerates-reproducing-.html
4. en.wikipedia.org/wiki/Buck_v._Bell
5. en.wikipedia.org/wiki/Lewis_Terman
6. www.theatlantic.com/education/archive/2014/11/modern-day-segregation-in-public-schools/382846
7. en.wikipedia.org/wiki/Arthur_Jensen
8. en.wikipedia.org/wiki/The_Bell_Curve#Policy_recommendations
9. www.slate.com/articles/briefing/articles/1997/01/the_bell_curve_flattened.html
10. www.psychometrics.cam.ac.uk/about-us/directory/beyond-the-flynn-effect
11. www.nytimes.com/2007/12/09/opinion/09nisbett.html?pagewanted=print
12. www.fbi.gov/news/stories/2014, www.ncjrs.gov/spotlight/hate_crimes/facts.html, www.splcenter.org
13. Human Genome Project: www.genome.gov/10001772

Also see
14. historynewsnetwork.org/article/1796
15. www.encyclopedia.com/topic/eugenics.aspx
16. plato.stanford.edu/entries/eugenics/#ShoHisEug

Problems with the Concept of Race
A Biological Perspective

3

Used with permission from the American Anthropological Association. Excerpts from their recommendations to the U.S. Census Bureau: "Race and Ethnic Standards for Federal Statistics and Administrative Reporting." www.aaanet.org > search "race" - www.learner.org/workshops/primarysources/census/docs/ombd.html

Anthropologically speaking, the concept of race is a relatively recent one. Historically, the term "race" was ascribed to groups of individuals who were categorized as biologically distinct. Rather than developing as a scientific concept, the current notion of "race" in the United States grew out of a European folk taxonomy or classification system sometime after Columbus sailed to the Americas. Increased exploration of far-away lands with people of different customs, languages, and physical traits clearly contributed to the developing idea. In these pre-Darwinian times the observed differences–biological, behavioral and cultural–were all considered to be products of creation by God. It was in this intellectual climate that the perceived purity and immutability of races originated. Perceived behavioral features and differences in intellect were inextricably linked to race and served as a basis for the ranking, in terms of superiority, of races.

Early natural history approaches to racial classification supported these rankings and the implications for behavior. For example, in the 18th century, Carolus Linneaus, the father of taxonomy and a European, described American Indians as not only possessing reddish skin, but also as choleric, painting themselves with fine red lines and regulated by custom. Africans were described as having black skin, flat noses and being phlegmatic, relaxed, indolent, negligent, anointing themselves with grease and governed by caprice. In contrast, Europeans were described as white, sanguine, muscular, gentle, acute, inventive, having long flowing hair, blue eyes, covered by close vestments and governed by law.

In the 1800s, the first "scientific" studies of race attempted to extract the behavioral features from the definition of race. However, racist interpretation remained. For example the origin of racial variation was interpreted as degeneration of the original "Caucasian" race (the idea of a Caucasian race is based on the belief that the most "perfect" skulls came from the Caucasus Mountains). Degeneration explained the development of racial differences and racial differences explained cultural development. Biology and behavior were used to gauge the degree of deterioration from the original race. Measures of intellect were an important part of these early studies. In some cases, the degree of facial prognathism, bumps on the skull…and cranial capacity were used as measures of intelligence. IQ is just the latest in the list of these so-called "definitive" features used to rank races.

The clearest data about human variation come from studies of genetic variation, which are clearly quantifiable and replicable. Genetic data show that, no matter how racial groups are defined, two people from the same racial group are about as different from each other as two people from any two different racial groups.

One of the basic principles about genetic transmission in families is that different variants are transmitted to different offspring independently…Fixed sets of traits are not transmitted across generations as many people assume. Rules like the "one drop of blood" rule show clearly how vague and social, rather than biological, are categorical terms for people.

…It is because people often share cultural identity and geographic ancestry that "race" or a system of terms for grouping people carries some information that can be useful for biomedical purposes (as in assigning resources for disease screening). For example, sickle cell hemoglobin is a health risk associated with black or African-descended populations and PKU or phenylketonuria is a health risk associated with white or European-descended populations…

"Race" as a concept is controversial because of the numerous instances in human history in which a categorical treatment of people, rationalized on the grounds of biology-like terms, have been used. Common examples of this include arguments about which "race" is more intelligent, better at mathematics or athletics, and so on. The ultimate use of categorical notions of race have occurred to achieve political ends, as in the Holocaust, slavery, and the [removal] of American Indian populations, that, while basically economic in motivation, has received support and rationale from biological language used to characterize groups…

The American Anthropological Association recognizes that classical racial terms may be useful for many people who prefer to use proudly such terms about themselves. The Association wishes to stress that if biological information is not the objective, biological-sounding terms add nothing to the precision, rigor, or factual basis of information being collected to characterize the identities of the American population. In that sense, phasing out the term "race," to be replaced with more correct terms related to ethnicity, such as "ethnic origins," would be less prone to misunderstanding.

Social and Cultural Aspects of "Race" and "Ethnicity"

Race and ethnicity both represent social or cultural constructs for categorizing people based on perceived differences in biology (physical appearance) and behavior. Although popular connotations of race tend to be associated with biology and those of ethnicity with culture, the two concepts are not clearly distinct from one another.

While diverse definitions exist, ethnicity may be defined as the identification with population groups characterized by common ancestry, language and custom. Because of common origins and intermarriage, ethnic groups often share physical characteristics which also then become a part of their identification—by themselves and/or by others. However, populations with similar physical appearance may have different ethnic identities, and populations with different physical appearances may have a common ethnic identity.

…today's ethnicities are yesterday's races. In the early 20th century in the US, Italians, the Irish, and Jews were all thought to be racial (not ethnic) groups whose members were inherently and irredeemably distinct from the majority white population. Today, of course, the situation has changed considerably. Italians, Irish, and Jews are now seen as ethnic groups that are included in the majority white population. The notion that they are racially distinct from whites seems far-fetched, possibly "racist." Earlier in the 20th century, the categories of Hindu and Mexican were included as racial categories in the Census. Today, however, neither would be considered racial categories.

Knowing the history of how these groups "became white" is an integral part of how race and ethnicity are conceptualized in contemporary America. The aggregated category of "white" begs scrutiny. It is important to keep in mind that the American system of categorizing groups of people on the basis of race and ethnicity, developed initially by a then-dominant white, European-descended population, served as a means to distinguish and control "non-white" populations in various ways.

…While both race and ethnicity are conceptualized as fixed categories, research demonstrates that individuals perceive their identities as fluid, changing according to specific contexts in which they find themselves.

…Census and common sense treat race and ethnicity as properties of an individual, ignoring the extent to which both are defined by the individual's **relation** to the society at large. Consider, for example, the way that racial and ethnic identity supposedly "predict" a range of social outcomes.

The typical correlation is that by virtue of being a member of a particular racial or ethnic group, imprisonment, poor health, poverty, and academic failure are more likely. Such an interpretation, while perhaps statistically robust, is structurally and substantively incomplete because it is not the individual's association with a particular racial or ethnic group that predicts these various outcomes but the attribution of that relationship by others that underlies these outcomes. For instance, a person is not more likely to be denied a mortgage because he or she is black (or Hispanic or Chinese), but because another person **believes** that he or she is black (or Hispanic or Chinese) and ascribes particular behaviors with that racial or ethnic category.

Recommendations

…The American Anthropological Association recommends the elimination of the term "race" from…the 2010 Census.

During the past 50 years, "race" has been scientifically proven to not be a real natural phenomenon. More specific, social categories such as "ethnicity" or "ethnic group" are more salient for scientific purposes and have fewer of the negative, racist connotations for which the concept of race was developed.

Yet the concept of race has become thoroughly—and perniciously—woven into the cultural and political fabric of the United States. It has become an essential element of both individual identity and government policy. Because so much harm has been based on "racial" distinctions over the years, correctives for such harm must also acknowledge the impact of "racial" consciousness among the U.S. populace, regardless of the fact that "race" has no scientific justification in human biology. Eventually, however, these classifications must be transcended and replaced by more non-racist and accurate ways of representing the diversity of the U.S. population.

This is the dilemma and opportunity of the moment. It is important to recognize the categories to which individuals have been assigned historically in order to be vigilant about the elimination of discrimination. Yet ultimately, the effective elimination of discrimination will require an end to such categorization, and a transition toward social and cultural categories that will prove more scientifically useful and personally resonant for the public than are categories of "race." Redress of the past and transition for the future can be simultaneously effected.

The American Anthropological Association recognizes that elimination of the term "race" in government parlance will take time to accomplish. However, the combination of the terms "race/ethnicity" …in the Census …will assist in this effort, serving as a bridge to the elimination of the term "race." ∎

A Long History of Affirmative Action—For Whites

Many middle-class white people, especially those of us from the suburbs, like to think that we got to where we are today by virtue of our merit—hard work, intelligence, pluck, and maybe a little luck. And while we may be sympathetic to the plight of others, we close down when we hear the words "affirmative action" or "racial preferences." We worked hard, we made it on our own, the thinking goes, why don't "they"? After all, the Civil Rights Act was enacted [over 50] years ago.

What we don't readily acknowledge is that racial preferences have a long, institutional history in this country—a white history. Here are a few ways in which government programs and practices have channeled wealth and opportunities to white people at the expense of others.

Early Racial Preferences

We all know the old history, but it's still worth reminding ourselves of its scale and scope. Affirmative action in the American "workplace" first began in the late 17th century when European indentured servants—the original source of unfree labor on the new tobacco plantations of Virginia and Maryland—were replaced by African slaves. In exchange for their support and their policing of the growing slave population, lower-class Europeans won new rights, entitlements, and opportunities from the planter elite.

White Americans were also given a head start with the help of the U.S. Army. The 1830 Indian Removal Act, for example, forcibly relocated Cherokee, Creeks and other eastern Indians to west of the Mississippi River to make room for white settlers. The 1862 Homestead Act followed suit, giving away millions of acres of what had been Indian Territory west of the Mississippi. Ultimately, 270 million acres, or 10% of the total land area of the United States, was converted to private hands, overwhelmingly white, under Homestead Act provisions.

The 1790 Naturalization Act permitted only "free white persons" to become naturalized citizens, thus opening the doors to European immigrants but not others. Only citizens could vote, serve on juries, hold office, and in some cases, even hold property. In this century, Alien Land Laws passed in California and other states, reserved farmland for white growers by preventing Asian immigrants, ineligible to become citizens, from owning or leasing land. Immigration restrictions further limited opportunities for nonwhite groups. Racial barriers to naturalized U.S. citizenship weren't removed until the McCarran-Walter Act in 1952, and white racial preferences in immigration remained until 1965.

In the South, the federal government never followed through on General Sherman's Civil War plan to divide up plantations and give each freed slave "40 acres and a mule" as reparations. Only once was monetary compensation made for slavery, in Washington, D.C. There, government officials paid up to $300 per slave upon emancipation—not to the slaves, but to local slaveholders as compensation for loss of property.

When slavery ended, its legacy lived on not only in the impoverished condition of Black people but in the wealth and prosperity that accrued to white slave owners and their descendants. Economists who try to place a dollar value on how much white Americans have profited from 200 years of unpaid slave labor, including interest, begin their estimates at $1 trillion. Jim Crow laws, instituted in the late 19th and early 20th century and not overturned in many states until the 1960s, reserved the best jobs, neighborhoods, schools and hospitals for white people.

The Advantages Grow, Generation to Generation

Less known are more recent government racial preferences, first enacted during the New Deal that directed wealth to white families and continue to shape life opportunities and chances. The landmark Social Security Act of 1935 provided a safety net for millions of workers, guaranteeing them an income after retirement. But the act specifically excluded two occupations: agricultural workers and domestic servants, who were predominately African American, Mexican, and Asian. As low-income workers, they also had the least opportunity to save for their retirement. They couldn't pass wealth on to their children. Just the opposite. Their children had to support them.

Like Social Security, the 1935 Wagner Act helped establish an important new right for white people. By granting unions the power of collective bargaining, it helped millions of white workers gain entry into the middle class over the next 30 years. But the Wagner Act permitted unions to exclude non-whites and deny them access to better paid jobs and union protections and benefits such as health care, job security and pensions. Many craft unions remained nearly all-white well into the 1970s. In 1972, for example, every single one of the 3,000 members of Los Angeles Steam Fitters Local #250 was still white.

But it was another racialized New Deal program, the Federal Housing Administration, that helped generate much of the wealth that so many white families enjoy today. These revolutionary programs made it possible for millions of average white Americans—but not others—to own a home for the first time. The government set up a national neighborhood appraisal system, explicitly tying mortgage eligibility to race. Integrated communities were *ipso facto* deemed a financial risk and made ineligible for home loans, a policy known today as "redlining." Between 1934 and 1962, the federal government backed $120 billion of home loans. More than 98% went to whites. Of the 350,000 new homes built with federal support in northern California between 1946 and 1960, fewer than 100 went to African Americans. These government programs made possible the new segregated white suburbs that sprang up around the country after World War II. Government subsidies for municipal services helped develop and enhance these suburbs further, in turn fueling commercial investments. Freeways tied the new suburbs to central business districts, but they often cut through and destroyed the vitality of non-white neighborhoods in the central city.

Today, Black and Latino mortgage applicants are still 60% more likely than whites to be turned down for a loan, even after controlling for employment, financial and neighborhood factors. According to the Census, whites are more likely to be segregated than any other group. As recently as 1993, 86% of suburban whites still lived in neighborhoods with a black population of less than 1%.

Reaping the Rewards of Racial Preference

One result of the generations of preferential treatment for whites is that a typical white family today has on average eight times the assets, or net worth, of a typical African American family, according to economist Edward Wolff. Even when families of the same income are compared, white families have more than twice the wealth of black families. Much of that wealth difference can be attributed to the value of one's home, and how much one inherited from parents.

But a family's net worth is not simply the finish line, it's also the starting point for the next generation. Those with wealth pass their assets on to their children—by financing a college education, lending a hand during hard times, or assisting with the down payment for a home. Some economists estimate that up to 80 percent of lifetime wealth accumulation depends on these intergenerational transfers. White advantage is passed down, from parent to child to grandchild. As a result, the racial wealth gap—and the head start enjoyed by whites— appears to have grown since the civil rights days.

In 1865, just after Emancipation, it is not surprising that African Americans owned 0.5 percent of the total worth of the United States. But by 1990, a full 125 years after the abolition of slavery, Black Americans still possessed only a meager 1 percent of national wealth.

Rather than recognize how "racial preferences" have tilted the playing field and given us a head start in life, many whites continue to believe that race does not affect our lives. Instead, we chastise others for not achieving what we have; we even invert the situation and accuse non-whites of using "the race card" to advance themselves.

Or we suggest that differential outcomes may simply result from differences in "natural" ability or motivation. However, sociologist Dalton Conley's research shows that when we compare the performance of families across racial lines who make not just the same income, but also hold similar net worth, a very interesting thing happens: many of the racial disparities in education, graduation rates, welfare usage and other outcomes disappear. The "performance gap" between whites and nonwhites is a product not of nature, but unequal circumstances.

Colorblind policies that treat everyone the same, no exceptions for minorities, are often counter-posed against affirmative action. But colorblindness today merely bolsters the unfair advantages that color-coded practices have enabled white Americans to long accumulate. It's a little late in the game to say that race shouldn't matter. ■

(c) California Newsreel, 2003, *RACE—The Power of an Illusion,* a three-part documentary series.
For information or video purchase: www.newsreel.org or 877-811-7495.
Visit the companion web site at www.PBS.org/Race

⑤ "I Don't See Color"

The following three articles address the concept of "colorblindness," an idea which may be well-intentioned, but which negates the life experiences of people of color. Even if an individual can ignore a person's skin color, society does not. Noticing color and speaking about race are not forms of racism. However, claiming to be "colorblind," insisting that "we're all just human," and refusing to have those sometimes difficult conversations—all contribute to the problem.

Let's Not Pretend We're Colorblind

Dr. William Howe, Chair, Connecticut Asian Pacific American Affairs Commission
OP-ED, Hartford Courant, June 16, 2014. Used with permission of the author.

Many well-meaning people talk about being colorblind or proudly claim that they are raising their children to ignore racial or other differences. I know they are sincere when they say those words, but I cringe each time I hear them. What are meant as good intentions can also have the opposite effect. For some, the term "colorblind" is heard as "I will pretend you are white and you pretend you are white and we will get along fine."

The intent is admirable—treat everyone equally regardless of skin color, ethnicity, religion or sexual orientation. Do not judge people based on superficial appearances. Get to know people as human beings and not as labels. Children are taught that "no one is better than anyone else." We are all equals. These are laudable beliefs but they hide some ugly truths.

For people of color, bias and discrimination are often a part of daily life…The downside of promoting colorblindness is an underlying message that one should ignore the injustices faced by so many.

…We must also teach our children the reality that society and the law does not treat us all equally. We must understand that some live a life of unearned privileges simply because of the color of their skin. A white teenager being followed around a store is not experiencing the same life as any black person similarly followed. My heart breaks every time I hear black parents talk about having to teach their sons never to run in public, especially with a parcel under their arms. When in a store, always keep your hands visible to avoid being accused of shoplifting. When confronted by the authorities, always remain polite and respectful no matter how badly you are treated.

I am Asian American. It is not uncommon for me to meet someone hesitant to speak to me because they are unsure if I speak English. How do you think Asian Americans born and raised in Connecticut feel when they are complimented on their good English?

… Black friends have relayed to me that they sometimes catch people wiping the palms of their hands on their pants after they have shaken hands. This is not a way to raise children for a global economy and diverse workforce…We are far from living a life where we can afford to be simply colorblind. ■

Colorblindness: the New Racism?

Dr. Afi-Odelia E. Scruggs, adjunct professor & journalist - www.aoscruggs.com. Reprinted with permission of Teaching Tolerance, a project of the Southern Poverty Law Center - www.tolerance.org

Kawania Wooten's voice tightens when she describes the struggle she's having at the school her son attends. When his class created a timeline of civilization, Wooten saw the Greeks, the Romans and the Incas. But nothing was said about Africa, even though the class has several African American students.

Wooten, who is black, spoke to the school's director, a white woman — who insisted that the omission wasn't racially biased. "Her first comment was, 'You know, we've just been following the curriculum. We're not talking about whether people are white or black.'...I said that the children have eyes and they can see. And I'd like them to see that our culture was a strong, viable culture."

That kind of story brings a groan from Mark Benn, a psychologist and adjunct professor at Colorado State University. He hears similar tales whenever he delivers lectures about race relations. Such incidents are examples of racial "colorblindness"—the idea that ignoring or overlooking racial and ethnic differences promotes racial harmony. Trainers and facilitators say colorblindness does just the opposite: folks who enjoy racial privilege are closing their eyes to the experiences of others.

...As the nation's demographics shift, the sight of a white teacher leaning over the desk of a brown or black student is likely to become more and more common. In order to be effective, teachers will have to learn about the cultural experiences of their students, while using these experiences as a foundation for teaching. The approach is called culturally relevant pedagogy.

But that is hard to do if a teacher doesn't see differences as valuable. That means the blinders have to come off, says Randy Ross, a senior equity specialist at the New England Equity Assistance Center..."I have never heard a teacher of color say 'I don't see color,'" Ross says. "There may be issues of cultural competence, but colorblindness is not one of them."

Such tunnel vision is the reason a teacher can omit Africa from a timeline of world civilizations, Ross says. Still, she cautions, the flaws of the colorblind approach run deeper than curriculum. Failure to see and acknowledge racial differences makes it difficult to recognize the unconscious biases everyone has. Those biases can taint a teacher's expectations of a student's ability and negatively influence a student's performance.

...Ross says a teacher who professes to be "colorblind" is not going to understand how unconscious biases can influence expectations, actions, and even the way a teacher addresses students of color.

After talking to her son's teacher, Kawania Wooten wondered whether her son was being harmed in just that way. ■

Colorblindness Is the New Racism

Lauren Rankin, http://mic.com/articles/55867/colorblindness-is-the-new-racism. Used with permission.

…Racism is a multi-faceted, complex framework, simultaneously covert and overt, both individual and systemic. It can be both an isolated incident and a structural fabric. And yet, by and large, Americans cling to the narrow idea that racism died along with the political correctness of the "N" word and the mass lynchings of blacks by white terrorists in the 20th century. Racism, they say, is a problem of the past. We have a black president. You are the racist ones, they say, because *you* keep talking about race. We don't see race. We don't have a race problem, they say.

We don't have a race problem, unless you count the school-to-prison pipeline in Mississippi that arrested and sentenced black students for infractions as small as wearing the wrong color socks. We don't have a race problem, unless you count New York City's Stop and Frisk program that has led to 400,000 NYPD encounters with innocent black and Latino New Yorkers.

We don't have a race problem, unless you count the fact that a black person is 3.73 times more likely to be arrested for marijuana possession than a white person, even though blacks and whites use marijuana at similar rates.

We don't have a race problem, unless you count the scores of white conservative leaders continually demanding our first black president prove his legitimacy and forcing him to release his birth certificate.

…We don't have a race problem, unless you count the innocent, unarmed 17-year-old black boy who was seemingly racially profiled, followed, shot, and killed, whose killer raised over $300,000 in online donations and then walked free with his life.

We don't have a race problem, unless you count the desperate lengths to which white people go to dismiss claims of racism from people of color and minimize the validity of their experiences. We don't have a race problem, except that, of course, we do.

Look around; those who claim that…racism is not a problem in the United States anymore, are almost always white…people who…feel all too comfortable declaring, over the overwhelmingly dissenting voices of people of color, that racism has ended. What a perfect encapsulation of white privilege and the entitlement that goes along with it.

"Colorblindness" sounds like a just and harmonious idea in theory, except that when put into practice, it discounts and erases the racial discrimination and oppression that people of color continually experience…Martin Luther King, Jr. envisioned a day where people were judged not on the color of their skin but on the content of their character, yes, but he also knew that we had to do the work to get to that point…We are applying colorblindness as a bandage before we even attempt to cleanse our painfully deep racist wound.

It's time to take off the blindfold, get off the merry-go-round, and tackle our racist past and present head on. ■

6) On Being Black in America

Abridged from a Facebook post by Brian Crooks and used with permission.
www.facebook.com/brian.crooks/posts/10103901923530909

Over the last few days I've done a lot of linking and reposting, but I haven't really done a lot of speaking about my personal experience to explain where I'm coming from. Please, bear with me for a few minutes. Hopefully, it'll help you understand.

The first time I was acutely aware of my Blackness, I was probably 6 or 7 years old. Like, before then obviously I knew I was Black, but I hadn't really had it put in my face like this. I used to go to daycare, and we went on a field trip to a water park. One of the other boys from the daycare came up to me and told me he was surprised I was going on the trip because his dad told him all colored people were afraid of the water since we sink to the bottom. He didn't know he was being offensive. He was just curious why someone who would sink to the bottom would want to go to a water park.

In elementary school, like many other Black people in my generation, I was the only Black kid in my class. I was in the gifted program. I've never been any good at math or science, but I was a really creative kid who loved history and telling stories. In third grade, the gifted program focused on the middle ages. I was in heaven. I loved learning about knights and castles and all that stuff. We had a group project where we had to give a short speech about something we'd learned during the year. All of the groups broke off to divvy up the work when my teacher came over to my group. Wouldn't it be "easier" and more fun for me if my group did our presentation as a rap? I'm eight years old. I have no history writing any kind of music, much less a full 3 or 4 minutes of rap verses for me and my teammates. But I tried. The other kids looked at me like, "What do you mean you don't know how to rap?" We ended up just doing it as a regular presentation like everybody else, and afterward my teacher came up to me and said, "I thought you guys were going to rap? I was looking forward to MC Brian." Again, she didn't know that she was making a racially insensitive statement. Why would she? It's not like she'd had deep conversations about how Black people feel about their Blackness, or the way Black people internalized the way White people feel about our Blackness.

From elementary school through middle school, I can't remember how many times the White kids asked if they could touch my hair. I'm not kidding when I say it happened pretty much once a week at least. At first, it didn't bother me. But eventually I felt like an exhibit in a petting zoo. I was a pretty shy kid. I was the only Black one, I was overweight, and I'd moved three times before I turned 10. So, rather than tell the White kids that no, they couldn't rummage through my hair, I just said yes and sat quietly while they marveled at how my hair felt.

My least favorite time of the year, every year, was February. Black History Month. Being the only Black kid in the class, I was the designated reader for the entire month. When it came time to read from our history books about slavery and the Triangle Trade Route, I was always the one who was chosen to read. When it came time to read about Jim Crow, it was my turn. George Washington Carver and the peanut? That sounds like a job for Brian. Booker T. Washington? Harriet Tubman? Surely Brian is the perfect choice for those passages. All the while, I felt the eyes of my fellow students on me. Again, I was already a shy kid. So, having an entire classroom of White kids stare at me while I explained what lynching and Black Codes were, was pretty mortifying.

Middle school is awkward for almost everybody. But when you're one of a handful of Black kids in a sea of judgmental, painfully self-conscious White kids, that awkwardness is magnified. I can remember being in 7th grade when a couple of girls who were always way too cool to talk to me ran up in the hallway and told me they had a girl for me to meet. I asked what she looked like. "You're really going to like her," they said. I met her near the end of the day. She was morbidly obese and about three shades darker than me. The popular girls, of course, decided that since we were both Black and overweight, we were a match made in heaven. I'm pretty sure they were aware that they were being jerks. But they were popular, I was a nerd, and the girl was new in school. I'm sure they told her they had a great guy for her too. We just stood there, both aware that we were the butt of their joke and aware that we didn't have the social cache to actually do anything about it.

In 8th grade, I went to a friend's house to jump on his trampoline. He had a couple of neighbors who were probably 6-or-7-year old girls. We're jumping on the trampoline and the girls were laughing while saying "Get off our property, Black boy." I don't think they knew how ugly they were being. But they'd clearly heard that phrase before. I wasn't even on their property. But it's fair to assume that at some point, someone in their house had said "Get off my property, Black boy."

When I was fifteen, I got my first "real" girlfriend, and she was White. I was living in an overwhelmingly White community and it's not like I was a heartthrob, so I was in no position to tell a girl who liked me that I was only interested in dating a Black girl. I might've never had a girlfriend if that was the line I drew. We were a good couple. We got along well and had similar interests and stuff. Her parents were divorced, but her mom and stepdad liked me. Then, her biological father found out I was Black. A week later, she called me crying and said we had to break up. Her dad didn't support her dating a Black person. So, my first heartbreak came as a direct result of racism.

In high school, I played football. There was a kid on the football team who I'd been friends with since middle school. When we were 16 or 17, he started referring to me as "The Whitest Black guy." It really pissed me off. I guess because I used proper grammar, wore clothes that fit, and listened to metal in addition to hip hop, it made me "White." Turns out, to be "authentically Black" means being a caricature of what a Black person should be, according to this suburban White kid. This is another case of me lacking the vocabulary at the time to express how that made me feel, but it's pretty messed up.

This kid (we're currently Facebook friends, so I hope he reads this and knows who I'm talking about) identified as Italian-American. I didn't call him "The most Anglo Italian guy" because he didn't bring homemade ravioli to school for lunch every day and play an accordion while growing a mustache.

I got pulled over a lot in high school. Like, a lot a lot. I had a Mazda. It was flashy and loud, but this was 2002 and everybody with a Japanese car was doing a Vin Diesel impression, so it's not like mine stood out. You can understand, then, why it was weird that I was routinely pulled over for a busted taillight. After all, that's the kind of thing I would've noticed and gotten fixed, especially if that taillight tended to burn out once a week or so. My parents had told me how to act when pulled over by the police, so of course I was all "Yes sir, no sir" every time it happened. That didn't stop them from asking me to step out of the car so they could pat me down or search for drugs. I didn't have a drop of alcohol until I was 21, but by that point I was an expert at breathalyzers and field sobriety tests.

On occasion, the officer was polite. But usually, they walked up with their hand on their gun and talked to me like I'd been found guilty of a grisly homicide earlier in the day. A handful of times, they'd tell me to turn off the car, drop the keys out the window, and keep my hands outside the vehicle before even approaching.

I went to the University of Iowa, which is a very White campus in a very White state. It's funny, because most of the people I met there who came from small-town Iowa were really excited to finally meet a Black person. They genuinely wanted a Black friend. It was nice. On the other hand, if I was in a bar and talking to a girl they didn't think I should be talking to, you'd be surprised to see how quickly some of these guys will call a complete stranger a nigger.

Once, when I came home from college, I was pulled over less than a block from my parents' house. It was late, probably about midnight or so, but I hadn't been drinking and it was winter so I wasn't speeding because it had snowed that day. The officer stepped out of his car with his gun drawn. He told me to drop the keys out the window, then exit the car with my hands up and step back toward him. I knew he was wrong, but I wasn't about to be shot to death down the street from my parents' house. He spent about 15 minutes searching my car while I stood handcuffed in the cold. My ID had my parents' address on it, but he still didn't think I lived there. I could tell he wanted to accuse me of having a fake ID. About a half hour after being pulled over, when he found nothing on me, nothing in my car, and nothing on my record, he reluctantly let me go.

In 2012, I went to watch the Iowa game at John Barleycorn on Clark Street in Chicago. I had gotten some t-shirts printed up and went to my car to get them so I could give them to my friends. While coming back, I saw a Michigan fan absolutely beating the hell out of a Nebraska fan (they were both White). I ran up into the fight and pulled the Michigan fan off the Nebraska fan. Dude's face was all bloody and messed up. The police were on the scene about 15 seconds later. Michigan and Nebraska both got to go home to "cool off," but I wound up handcuffed and sitting on the curb. There were at least a dozen witnesses there who tried to tell the officer that I was just trying to break up the fight. After 15 minutes, the officer removed the handcuffs and let me go. He said if he ever saw me on Clark Street again, we'd have a problem.

I could go on and on and on about this. I could tell you about the coworker who thought it was funny to adopt a stereotypical Black accent to apologize that we weren't going to have fried chicken and cornbread at our company Christmas party. I could tell you about the time I gave my floor mate a haircut and he "thanked" me by saying he'd let a negro cut his hair any day of the week. I could tell you about leaving a bar heartbroken and fighting tears when the Trayvon Martin verdict came out, only to see a couple of middle-aged White guys high-fiving and saying "he got what he deserved," right outside. These are only a handful of the experiences I've had in my 31 years.

I've never had a Black boss. I played football from middle school through senior year of high school and only had one Black coach that whole time. I've had two Black teachers in my entire life. I've never been to a Black doctor, or a Black dentist. I've never been pulled over by a Black police officer. What I'm trying to explain is that, in 31 years, I've seen three Black people in a position of authority. Think about what that does to the psyche of a growing young man.

I don't want to hear that you're "sorry I had these experiences." Because it's not just me. This is what it means to be Black in America. I appreciate that you're sorry for me, but I'm not seeking your sorrow. I just want you to understand that this is real. We're not exaggerating it, and we're not making it up. White people often say that we make everything about race. That's because, for us, damn near every-thing IS about race. It's always been that way. When I have a great phone interview, but go for my in-person interview only to be told that the position has been filled, how am I supposed to know that's not just because they expected a White Iowa graduate to show up for the interview? When I have an especially attentive employee keep checking in with me at the mall, how am I supposed to know they're shooting for employee of the month, not watching me to make sure I'm not stealing? What do you think it's like seeing Confederate flags on cars and flagpoles in northern states, only to have someone tell me I'm being too sensitive for not liking it?

When we say "Black Lives Matter," understand what that actually means. We aren't saying that ONLY Black lives matter. We're saying "Black lives matter TOO." For the entire history of this country, Black lives have not mattered. If a Black person kills another Black person, and we have it on tape, the killer goes to jail. If a White police officer kills a Black person and we have it on tape, the entire judicial system steps up to make sure that officer doesn't go to jail. It doesn't matter whether the Black person was holding a toy gun in a Walmart, or whether the Black person was a 12-year-old kid playing with a BB gun in an empty park. The police union steps up to say the officer was fearing for his life, just worried about making it home that night.

IF, by some miracle, an indictment is handed down, no jury is actually going to convict that officer. That's what we mean when we say Black Lives Matter. If we can have video evidence that an officer pulled up, jumped out of his car, shot a 12-year-old to death less than 2 seconds after arriving on the scene, administered no first aid, tackled and hand-cuffed the boy's sister when she arrived, and then falsified a police report to say that the boy pointed a gun at him and that he only shot when the boy refused several orders to drop his weapon, and STILL not get an indictment; or if a White man sees a 14-year-old Black boy in his neighborhood, follows him in his car, ignores orders not to engage him, then gets into a fight with him and shoots him in the chest and is found not guilty, why should we expect ANYBODY to go to jail for killing us? It's just not realistic. It's a fairy tale.

That is why Black people are in such pain right now. The deaths are bad enough. But having the feeling that nobody will ever actually be held accountable for the deaths is so much worse. And then watching as the police union, the media, and conservative politicians team up to imagine scenarios where the officer did nothing wrong, and then tell those of us who are in pain that our pain is wrong, unjustified, and all in our heads, just serves to twist the knife.

If you read all this, I really, really want to say thank you. I know it was a lot to get through. But this is real. This is me. This is what my life is and has been. And I'm not alone. ∎

7 Learning About Racial Differences and Similarities

From Anti-Bias Curriculum: Tools for empowering Young Children (p. 30-35)
by Louise Derman-Sparks & the ABC Task Force, Washington, D.C. Used with permission.

"Why am I called White if my skin is tan?"
"Will darker skin colors come off in the bathtub?"
"If her mom is black and her dad is white, why isn't she gray?"

> A considerable body of research demonstrates that children in the U.S. are aware, at a *very* early age…of racial differences. Many are also aware of racism. Yet the silence of the vast majority of textbooks, which are used to train teachers and other professionals, reflects and perpetuates a prevailing majority culture ideology—that children are "color-blind…" This ideology further assumes that if adults don't talk with children about it, children will grow up to be non-prejudiced adults. Denial and avoidance, then, appear to be the main techniques for dealing with one of the most pervasive and crucial problems of U.S. society…

Young children are very open to developing anti-bias attitudes and behaviors if adults actively counteract the negative impact of sexism, racism and [ableism]. Empowerment starts early. Effective anti-bias teaching means listening for and using spontaneous moments. However, adult-planned activities that help children directly address their misconceptions, discomforts and unfair behaviors are also essential….Children need guidance in sorting out their ideas and feelings so that racism cannot harm their self-concept or teach them to reject others. For children of groups oppressed by racism, the task is learning to struggle against its impact. For white children, it is learning to be anti-racist…The first step in this process is to accept the fact that a process is required.

GOALS

1. To encourage children to ask about their own and others' physical characteristics
2. To provide children with accurate, developmentally appropriate information
3. To enable children to feel pride, but not superiority, about their racial identity
4. To enable children to develop ease with and respect for physical differences
5. To help children become aware of our shared physical characteristics—what makes us all human beings

Preschoolers are aware of variations and wonder where they fit in.

Skin color is a frequent focus of interest. Coloring with brown crayon, Donald (3½) announces at large, "I'm brown too. I'm about as brown as this crayon." "Yes," appropriately responds his teacher, "your skin is a beautiful brown." Positively acknowledging a child's skin color is an important step in a child's developing concept of who he is and how he feels about himself.

Another teacher might have said, "Oh, it doesn't matter what color you are; we are all people," diverting Donald's attention from his skin color. This is an inappropriate response, based on the mistaken notion that noticing skin color causes prejudice. In fact, that response could teach Donald to think that there is something wrong with his skin color.

Cindy (4) asks her teacher matter-of-factly, "If I'm Black and White, and Tiffany is Black and White, how come her skin is darker?" "Well," her teacher explains, "each of you has a mommy who is Black and a daddy who is White, but when the colors of Black and White mix together it doesn't always look the same. Sometimes it is lighter brown and sometimes darker brown.

All the colors are beautiful."

During story time, Hector (4) leans over and touches Jamal's hair. Jamal pushes his hand away. Their teacher intervenes: "Hector, have you ever touched hair like Jamal's before?" Hector shakes his head no. Jamal interjects, "He didn't ask me if it's OK." Teacher: "Would it be all right if Hector asked first?" Jamal: "Yes." (He turns to Hector.) "Ask me and then you can touch it." "Then I want to touch your hair." Teacher: "Yes, it's fun to touch and learn about each other's hair as long as we ask first. Did Jamal's hair feel the same as or different than your hair?"

Hector and the rest of the children are having an important lesson—how to respectfully learn from each other. If Jamal had said it wasn't all right for Hector to touch his hair, then the teacher might have said, "We have to respect what Jamal says. There are other ways to learn about each other's hair." In this way, he supportingly acknowledges as OK both Hector's curiosity and Jamal's rights.

"Craig's eyes go like this," says 4-year-old Ruth, pulling her eyes up. "They look funny." Her teacher replies: "Craig's eyes are not funny; they have a different shape than yours. Craig's eyes are the same shape as his family's eyes, just as your eyes are shaped like your family's. Both of your eye shapes are fine and both are good for seeing. It is OK to ask questions about how people look. It is not OK to say they look funny. That hurts their feelings."

If Craig had been adopted by a non-Asian family, then the teacher might say, "Craig's eyes are shaped like the millions of people who live in the country he came from," and follow up with more about Craig's country of origin.

CAUTION

When children ask questions about racial physical characteristics:
- Do not ignore.
- Do not change the subject.
- Do not answer indirectly.

> If you are uncomfortable, identify what gets in the way of your responding directly, matter-of-factly, simply.

Children want to know how they got their color, hair and eye characteristics.

"How do people get their color?" asks 3-year-old Heather. "What are your ideas?" her teacher responds. "Well, I was wondering about pens. With pens you can put red or blue or brown on your skin if you want to." Teacher: "I'm glad you are trying to figure things out, but that's not how people get their skin color. We get our skin color from our mommies and daddies. Your skin is the same color as mine. Marizza's skin color is like her mommy and daddy's. Denise's skin is lighter brown because she's a mixture of her mommy's white skin and her daddy's black skin."

Respect children's ideas while also giving them accurate information. Rebecca, who has been playing with Miyoko, a child recently arrived from Japan, asks the teacher: "Can you make my eyes like Miyoko's? If I learn to speak Japanese, will I have eyes like hers?" Her teacher explains that her eye shape cannot be changed, even if she learns to speak Japanese. "We get our eyes from how our parents look; we learn to talk the way our parents talk. Miyoko's parents speak Japanese, so she speaks Japanese. Your parents speak English, so you speak English."

A few days later, the teacher sees Rebecca trying to make her eyes look Japanese. She says, "Rebecca, it isn't polite to pull on your eyes; Miyoko might think you are making fun of her."

Children wonder if skin color, hair and eyes remain constant.

"Last summer I got to be as dark as Maria," [says Robin]. "So then I was Mexican, now I'm not." Teacher: "Yes, our skin color can get darker when we play a lot in the sun, and lighter when we don't. That doesn't mean we can change our skin color any way we want. Even when your skin color looked like Maria's you still weren't Mexican. Maria is [of Mexican heritage] because her mom and dad and grandparents are Mexican. You [have Irish heritage] because your parents and grandparents are Irish." Robin: "But I want to be just like Maria. She's my best friend." Teacher: "It's great that you and Maria are best friends. I know you have a lot of fun playing together at school and at home. You don't have to be just the same to be best friends."

"I'm going to make my eyes straight and blue," 4-year-old Kim tells her teacher. "Why do you want to change your lovely eyes?" her teacher asks wonderingly. Kim: "It's prettier." Teacher: "Kim, I don't think straight eyes are prettier than yours are. Your mommy and grandma and grandpa don't think so either. We like you just the way you are, with your beautiful, dark brown eyes shaped just as they are. Why do you think straight and blue eyes are prettier?" Kim: "Sarah said I had ugly eyes. She likes Julie's better." Teacher: "Sarah is wrong to say you have ugly eyes. It's not true and it is unfair and hurtful to say so. In this classroom we respect how everyone looks. Let's go and talk with her about it."

Children of color, more often than White children, may verbalize not liking the color, texture or shape of their skin, hair or eyes. This happens because racism attacks children of color's physical characteristics. It is very important to address the child's feelings immediately and to assure her that how she is, is just right, that her family and teacher love her as she is, and that people who think her looks are not OK are wrong. Help the child understand that there are millions of people who have the same skin color or eye shape as they do, even if she is numerically a minority in the class. The goals are to facilitate children's awareness that their racial identity does not change, to help them understand that they are part of a large group with similar characteristics (they are not "different"), and to foster their desire to be exactly who they are.

As their classification ability expands, so too will their further understanding.

"I'm not Black," Tiffany, a dark-skinned Black child, kept saying during a discussion about skin color. Her teacher, worried about her self-concept, tried talking with Tiffany but she kept insisting, "I'm not Black." Talking with her parents that evening to figure out what to do, the teacher learned to her embarrassment that they use the term Afro-American, not Black. As soon as her teacher used the term Tiffany recognized, her self-concept was fine.

This incident highlights the importance of finding out from parents the terms they use and what and how they are teaching their child about her racial/ethnic identity. However, the teacher's concern and immediate phone call to Tiffany's parents were appropriate, even if her interpretation of the situation lacked a vital piece of information.

A Navajo man visits Joshua's childcare center to talk about his life. He is dressed in jeans, plaid shirt, "cowboy" hat and boots. Joshua (3½) calls out, "You're not an Indian." His teacher, much embarrassed, says, "Yes, he is. He is a Navajo Indian. Why do you think he isn't an Indian?" "He's not wearing feathers," Joshua replies. "People who are Indians wear many different kinds of clothes. Many do not wear feathers. We need to learn more about this," the teacher responds.

Though adults often feel embarrassed when children blurt out questions and comments in the presence of those they are talking about, it is very important to overcome the embarrassment and be an educator. ∎

(8) Ten Things Everyone Should Know About Race

Our eyes tell us that people look different. No one has trouble distinguishing a Czech from a Chinese, but what do those differences mean? Are they biological? Has race always been with us? How does race affect people today? There's less—and more—to race than meets the eye:

1. **Race is a modern idea**. Ancient societies, like the Greeks, did not divide people according to physical distinctions, but according to religion, status, class, even language. The English language didn't even have the word 'race' until it turns up in 1508 in a poem by William Dunbar referring to a line of kings.

2. **Race has no genetic basis.** Not one characteristic, trait or even one gene distinguishes all the members of one so-called race from all the members of another so-called race.

3. **Human subspecies don't exist.** Unlike many animals, modern humans simply haven't been around long enough or isolated enough to evolve into separate subspecies or races. Despite surface appearances, we are one of the most similar of all species.

4. **Skin color really is only skin deep.** Most traits are inherited independently from one another. The genes influencing skin color have nothing to do with the genes influencing hair form, eye shape, blood type, musical talent, athletic ability or forms of intelligence. Knowing someone's skin color doesn't necessarily tell you anything else about him or her.

5. **Most variation is within, not between, "races."** Of the small amount of total human variation, 85% exists within any local population, be they Italians, Kurds, Koreans or Cherokees. About 94% can be found within any continent. That means two random Koreans may be as genetically different as a Korean and an Italian.

6. **Slavery predates race.** Throughout much of human history, societies have enslaved others, often as a result of conquest or war, even debt, but not because of physical characteristics or a belief in natural inferiority. Due to a unique set of historical circumstances, ours was the first slave system where all the slaves shared similar physical characteristics.

7. **Race and freedom evolved together.** The U.S. was founded on the radical new principle that "All men are created equal." But our early economy was based largely on slavery. How could this anomaly be rationalized? The new idea of race helped explain why some people could be denied the rights and freedoms that others took for granted.

8. **Race justified social inequalities as natural.** As the race idea evolved, white superiority became "common sense" in America. It justified not only slavery but also the extermination of Indians, exclusion of Asian immigrants, and the taking of Mexican lands by a nation that professed a belief in democracy. Racial practices were institutionalized within American government, laws and society.

9. **Race isn't biological, but racism is still real.** Race is a powerful social idea that gives people different access to opportunities and resources. Our government and social institutions have created advantages that disproportionately channel wealth, power and resources to white people. This affects everyone, whether we are aware of it or not.

10. **Colorblindness will not end racism**. Pretending race doesn't exist is not the same as creating equality. Race is more than stereotypes and individual prejudice. To combat racism, we need to identify and remedy social policies and institutional practices that advantage some groups at the expense of others. ∎

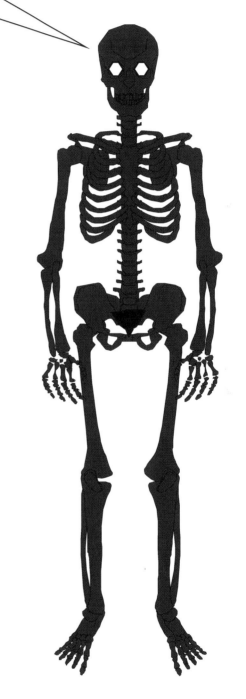

HOORAY FOR SKIN

by Susan Engle

Rejoice and celebrate the skin
That keeps the veins and muscles in,
That keeps the cold and germies out.
That is what skin is all about.

Suppose that when you got your skin,
You found the skin side outside-in.
So when you talk to Mrs. Jones,
Your eyes meet over fat and bones,
And tissues, blue and white and red,
That stretch from toe to hand to head.
It makes me glad to have a skin
To keep the outside boneside-in.

Now there are folks who would be mad
If our insides were all they had
To tell all kinds of folks apart.
Maybe they'd learn to read the heart
Instead of judging from a hue
If one man's false and one man's true.

Let's all join hands and feast our eyes
On skins of every shape and size,
Of every tone of gold or white,
Of luscious black, of dark or light,
Of every shade that folks come in.
Rejoice and celebrate the skin.

Notes: _____

_____

_____

_____

_____

_____

_____

_____

_____

_____

_____

_____

_____

_____

_____

_____

_____

_____

_____

_____

_____

_____

Name Power

Taking Pride and Control in Defining Ourselves

By Ferdinand M. De Leon and Sally Macdonald. Used with permission of The Seattle Times.

[0] All these many years after the nation's wrenching confrontations over civil rights, you can still hear the clenched fist in Rick Olguin's voice as he declares, "I am a Chicano."

And the firm resolve in Maxine Chan's as she corrects someone who has just called her an Oriental, "I am not a rug."

And the calm certainty in Nona Brazier's as she talks about abandoned labels and concludes, "I will always refer to myself as an African American."

Few things are as fundamental as what we call ourselves. The labels we use affect how others perceive us and how we see ourselves; they shape how we see others and how we want to be seen by them; they are used by those in power to define the rest even as they struggle to define themselves.

They shape who we are. Little wonder then, that when the names we have always used for ourselves and for others start to change, as they are doing, we feel a tremor down the spine of our collective national consciousness.

Is it African American or is it black? Should we use Hispanic or Latino? Native American or American Indian? What about white? What about Asian American?

Then comes the underlying question that - depending on who does the asking and what spurred the question - can inspire understanding or provoke outrage: "Why can't we all just be Americans?"

[1] LANGUAGE IS POLITICAL

Today, more of us than ever come from somewhere else. More of us than ever have brown or black skins, not white ones. More of us than ever are demanding that the names people call us are respectful ones, ones we have chosen to best describe ourselves.

"Language is political," says Guadalupe Friaz, an assistant professor of ethnic studies at the University of Washington. "When we talk about language we're talking about the relationships between people, and what people call each other reflects whatever tension and anxiety that society is going through."

We've fought for power among ourselves for generations, and words have been a frequent weapon. We sling epithets that bruise as much as bricks and police batons. Nicknames for whole groups of people slide from slang to slur, gathering the power to maim psychologically.

Some labels retain for generations the power to call up a host of stereotypes that dig and slice and kill the spirit.

But sometimes the group at the receiving end of that abuse reclaims a label, like "black," effectively changing it from a negative term to a positive and proud one.

"Change is constant," Friaz says. "Group relationships always change, so of course terminology is going to change. As people of color we don't have power, and we haven't had the power to name."

But that, too, is changing.

[2] BLACK OR AFRICAN AMERICAN?

In 1967, Larry Gossett stopped using Negro and became black. Today, he's African American. Gossett, executive director of the Central Area Motivation Program, was then involved in the civil-rights struggle, and the switch came as the black-power and black-pride movement gained steam.

"We were defining black as beautiful and not as something ugly," Gossett says. "It had a profound inspirational impact on the youth of the '60s."

The new label was a rejection of the labels imposed by whites and the labels of his parents' generation - a radical reclaiming of a word that had been viewed as a slur.

"It was revolutionary and emotionally wrenching because we had parents saying, 'We've been Negroes and coloreds all our lives. Why are you calling yourselves black?'" Gossett says. "Black, in America and in the English language, had such a negative connotation that it scared our parents."

The changes in the labels used by or for African Americans over the course of the country's history reflect the struggles between the dominant culture and other groups.

For centuries, negro – in the lower case – was the accepted label. But after Reconstruction there was a push by black leaders and the black press to give dignity to the name by capitalizing it - an effort that took 50 years.

In the 1900s, "colored" competed with Negro as the preferred group name, and it lives on today in the name of the National Association for the Advancement of Colored People, founded in 1910. Afro-American was first proposed in 1880, but it didn't catch on.

Eventually Negro emerged as the preferred name, surviving until the late 1960s, when it was rejected by younger black people because of its associations with slavery.

Three years ago, Gossett decided it was time for him to make another switch - this time to African American.

"How you refer to yourselves as a people has social, historical and cultural significance," Gossett says. "I'm from the current school of thought which says that African American comes closest to describing who we are as a people."

The change is rooted in the political growth of the African-American community, Gossett says, and was also prompted in part by a sense of identification with Africa - especially the struggles of black South Africans.

For Gossett, it was again the reclaiming of a word that had been tarnished.

Today Gossett uses African American and black interchangeably, but he believes African American will prevail. Although most people still use black, many community leaders agree.

For Nona Brazier, the switch to African American happened further back. Like Gossett, Brazier used black as a reaction to her parents' use of Negro. But by the end of the 1960s, she had started to use African American.

"I often refer to black folks and the black community, but I never refer to myself as a black American," says Brazier, who is co-owner of Northwest Recovery Systems, a recycling firm.

Brazier's preference for African American is rooted in her direct ties to Africa. She has a business in Nigeria and feels an attachment to the land from which her ancestors came.

"The fact that I refer to myself as an African American reflects my time," Brazier says. "It's based on myself, my life and times, and even if other labels emerge, I will always refer to myself as an African American."

"It doesn't matter what others call you, but it's very important what you call yourself."

[3] NATIVE AMERICANS OR AMERICAN INDIANS?

As every child learns in grade school, Christopher Columbus sailed the ocean blue to find India, and when he arrived in the New World, he mistakenly named the people Indians.

Yet the name survives today. And to Joseph Brown, a Lakota elder who has worked with the homeless and street kids, Indian is just fine.

"The word Indian identifies us," Brown says. "Indian covers a lot. A lot of Indians don't like to be called Indian because they're trying to be white men and they're prejudiced against themselves."

But for others, especially those who are younger, Native American is the preferred label because it rejects the tragic historical associations that the word Indian carries.

"The idea of calling people Native Americans appeals to me because we are native - more so than any other group," says Allethia Allen, an assistant professor of social work at the UW. "I would prefer that because the name Indian comes from Columbus."

Others say there are no right or wrong choices.

"I think the majority feels comfortable with the word Indian," says Cecil James, a resource-management worker for the Yakima fisheries. "Each individual has their own definition of how they want to be called. When I talk in public, I identify myself as an Indian of the Yakima Nation, but it should be up to each person to decide."

Allen, who is half Native American and part black and white, says she hasn't eliminated Indian from her own vocabulary.

"People tend to do what the majority does," Allen

says. "But people are getting much more distinctive about what they say about their heritage and their customs and very, very identified with their bloodline."

While there seems to be no overwhelming majority for using either Indian or Native American, most agree that using tribal affiliations is usually preferred.

"Traditionally, among Native Americans, we identified each other by our tribal affiliation, and very often people greet each other that way," says Allen, who is Mohawk and Mohican. "To me, the more clearly a person is described in terms of heritage, the better it is."

Robert Eaglestaff, the principal of American Indian Heritage School in Seattle says: "Most Indian tribes describe themselves as The People or human beings. The Lakotas, my tribe, means the friendly people. The others are labels, and I take labels for what they're worth - with a grain of salt. But I know who I am."

[4] WHAT ABOUT ASIAN AMERICANS?

Not long ago, Ron Chew, director of the Wing Luke Museum in Seattle's International District, was interviewing an elderly woman in Sequim about some of the Chinese people who settled on the Olympic Peninsula in the early days. She described them as Chinamen.

"I didn't correct her," he says. "She grew up in another era and was frozen in time. Maybe in her time and her place that was not a derogatory term. But

language evolves. What might be appropriate at one time might not be at another."

Chinaman is not OK anymore, and neither is Oriental, although it's a term still used by some older Asians and many whites.

"Oriental has a negative connotation," says Maxine Chan, a Chinese American who works with the community for the Seattle Police Department. "It's very much the Fu Manchu, Suzy Wong thing. It speaks about the 'yellow peril,' and the 'yellow horde.' If someone calls me that, I just say I'm not a rug."

While Asian American is all right, most people of Asian heritage would rather be identified by the country of their origin.

"Asian Americans need to be divided into Japanese Americans or Chinese Americans or Korean Americans - just because they want to be," says Setsuko Buckley, a Japanese language teacher and multicultural education expert at Western Washington University in Bellingham. "Even Southeast Asians are different from each other - Vietnamese, Thai, Cambodian - and they should have the option of being called what they want."

Tomie Rogers, a UW medical student, says she's "half Japanese, half Swedish-Irish."

When she was younger, new friends often thought - based on her almond-shaped eyes and tall stature - she must be Native American. "I don't really take offense to whatever people call me," she says. "I don't really have much ethnic feeling, and

I don't even know how I'm listed as a student. I often mark the 'other' box."

Being considered Asian poses a problem for some Filipinos and Pacific Islanders: They aren't from the Asian continent and feel they shouldn't be put in that category. Many Filipinos have the Catholic religion, Spanish surnames and some cultural vestiges of their colonial days.

"Our biggest problem in the Filipino community, besides economics, is an identity crisis," says Fred Cordova, a historian, author and manager of the UW information-services office.

"We've never had a chance to identify ourselves. The majority of our community here is made up of immigrants now, and they're very different from the ones who have been here a long time."

Most of the Asian and Latino groups are trying to deal with the chaos created by large waves of immigrants in recent years. As each new group begins to settle itself in the United States, another new group comes pouring in.

Many never come to think of themselves as full-fledged U.S. citizens and neither do their children. They continue to use the ethnic label they arrived with, identifying themselves as, say, Chinese - not Chinese American.

"A lot of us just don't put on the American tag," says Chew. "For most of us, it's understood that we're here, and for some, particularly the older generation, when they say American, they mean white."

[5] HISPANIC, LATINO OR CHICANO?

Like Asians, people whose ethnic roots are in Latin America most often identify themselves by the country of their forebears – Mexican American, Cuban American. If they have to be inclusive, they'll be Latino.

Even that is "an umbrella term that will suffer the same complications" with age as other broad ethnic identifications, says the UW's Guadalupe Friaz. "If you have to have a broad term, it's OK. At least it's not Eurocentric."

If Lorenzo Alvarado is given the choice of Hispanic to mark on a document, he'll say that's what he is. But when he marks the box that way, he feels he's losing his real heritage somehow. "I may be in America, but I'm a Mexican," says the Kent School District math teacher.

Hispanic - a tag made up by census workers to identify Latin Americans, Caribbean Islanders and Spaniards – is considered by most of those it would describe as too broad, irritatingly bureaucratic or just plain unacceptable.

"My understanding is there is no place called Hispanica," says Eduardo Diaz, a social-service administrator. "I think it's degrading to be called something that doesn't exist. Even Latino is a misnomer. We don't speak Latin."

Friaz calls herself a Chicana, a term - like a raised fist of defiance - that gathered power during the anti-war and civil-rights movements. Although the term has lost some of its punch, many baby boomers who called themselves Chicanos (or Chicana, the feminine form) in their youth still do today.

For some Mexican Americans, the term became a survival tool to replace Mexican, which had become tainted with racism, says Rick Olguin, a UW ethnic-studies assistant professor. Now Mexican is back in favor.

Javier Almaya, a native Colombian who has been in the United States for 10 years, is reasonably comfortable calling himself a Latino. But, like many Latin Americans, he considers himself a mestizo - a mixture of European and Indian ancestry. It's a term that's used widely in Central and South America but isn't readily recognized in this country.

Such complexity is the rule in discussions of ethnic labels for Latinos.

Consider the employees of Diaz's Seattle office: Diaz is the assistant manager of the King County Guardian Ad Litem program, a court advocacy program for children. A Puerto Rican who grew up in the Bronx in New York City, he says he feels degraded if he's called a Hispanic.

But Cathy Ortiz, the office's support staff supervisor, whose grandparents still live in Mexicali, Baja California, says although Hispanic is OK with her, she'd rather be called an American of Mexican descent.

And Rita Amaro, an office worker, is a third-generation Mexican American who says people can call her Latina, although the word reminds her of "kind of an island, like Puerto Rico or Cuba."

[6] MINORITY, NON-WHITE OR PEOPLE OF COLOR?

When whites were clearly the dominant group in this country, it was easy to divide the population into majority and minority.

Not the most sensitive division, but a handy one for whites that reflected the existing power dynamics and neatly summed up who had the power and numbers and who didn't.

But as whites lose their numerical dominance, and non-white immigrants continue to come into the country, the racial makeup of the nation becomes even more complex.

The balance is shifting. At the current rate of growth, the groups we consider minorities will collectively become the majority in this country in about 2050, according to recent projections by the Population Reference Bureau, a nonprofit Washington, D.C., agency that studies demographic trends. The bureau based its projection on 1990 census figures.

There has long been a debate over what to call people who aren't white. In 1962, in The Negro History Bulletin, Eldridge Cleaver wrote of the term non-white:

"The very words that we use indicate that we have set a premium on the Caucasian ideal of beauty. When discussing interracial relations, we speak of 'white people' and 'non-white people.' Notice that that particular choice of words gives precedence to 'white people' . . . making them a center – a standard – to which "non-white" bears a negative relation. Notice the different connotation when we turn around and say "colored" and 'non-colored' or 'black' or 'non-black.'"

These days much of the discussion centers on the phrase "people of color," an alternative that has emerged in recent years. It has generated strong reactions - but so far little consensus among those to whom the phrase would be applied.

"I don't like the term 'people of color,' " says Almaya, a health educator with the AIDS Prevention Project. "It doesn't give us any definition. It could be a person from Colombia or a person from Samoa, and they don't really have anything in common at all."

But Olguin likes the phrase and argues that it was significantly different from the now discredited "colored people."

"It's viewing it from the top instead of the bottom," he says. "'Colored people' says 'inferior,' and to be a colored person is to define a people by their color. But people of color are persons with other attributes."

But the changes won't come easily, and those who would claim the power to name themselves - and do away with long-entrenched labels - should expect resistance, says UW Professor Haig Bosmajian, whose book "The Language of Oppression" explores the power of language.

Bosmajian says opposition usually comes from two groups: those who need to be persuaded that there is a problem, and those who have a psychological stake in maintaining their power and not acquiescing to the new labels.

"It's more than etiquette, it's power," he says.

[7] WHITE, CAUCASIAN OR EURO-AMERICAN?

White people don't tend to think much about what they're called. Since they're already the majority, they see no need to label themselves.

"I don't think of it the way a black person would call himself black," says Nick Wilson, a Metro bus driver. "I think my grandparents were Irish, but I don't really even know. The only thing I can tell you about one of my grandfathers is that he was from Texas. Come to think of it, he was a Texan."

"I don't think about it at all," says Jerry Edwards, a Seattle yacht broker. "And I guess that's as much an indication of the situation as anything.

"It points out how privileged we are compared to other racial groups." When pressed to make a choice between white and Caucasian, Edwards dislikes both. "Caucasian is too antiseptic somehow, and white is too racial."

"It's easy in America to be white," says Pier van den Berghe, a UW sociology and anthropology professor. "It's easy for whites to forget they're white. But it's impossible for blacks to forget they're black."

When van den Berghe is asked to check a box with his ethnic background, he marks 'Other' or 'African American.' He's white, but he can do that, he says, because he was born in South Africa.

In the Southwest, whites are used to being called Anglos. But Anglo, introduced by Mexicans, means English. And many whites point out that England is not their homeland.

Many white people dislike being called Caucasian. Van den Berghe calls it "a pseudo-ethnic label" and he finds it "profoundly objectionable."

Most modern scholars no longer use racial divisions. Genetically, people are people, and any differences between them only skin deep. Friaz, the UW ethnic-studies professor, calls whites Euro-Americans, a term many whites consider contrived and unnecessary and in some cases erroneous.

Friaz believes whites should start their own discussion of heritage.

"Everyone has an ethnicity," she says. "Euro-Americans have to start seeing themselves as ethnics. Most Euro-Americans are not proud of who they are. I ask my white students about their ethnicity and they say, 'I guess I'm American.' They say it in an apologetic way."

This denial of cultural background is something that wasn't widely seen until World War I, Friaz says. Until then, most whites sent their children to language schools after their regular classes to preserve their culture.

But with the onset of the war, becoming "American" meant proving your loyalty by rejecting all ties to other lands.

"This is one of the few countries in the world that is willfully ignorant – which is a worse kind of ignorance," says the UW's Olguin. "In the rest of the world it's a virtue to speak different languages. Here if you speak three languages you're trilingual, and if you speak two languages you're bilingual, and if you speak one language, you're American."

[8] WHY CAN'T WE ALL JUST BE AMERICANS?

It seems like a simple enough question, but it can be fraught with insensitivity and misunderstanding depending on who hears it and who asks.

At best, it's a naive, idealistic attempt to say, "Why can't we quit categorizing each other?" If we call each other the same thing, it insists, other differences will dissolve.

But Friaz and some other people of color hear the question this way: "Why do you have to keep emphasizing your ethnicity, your color? Why can't you be white like us?"

Those questions release a flood of perceived insensitivities: Why don't you adopt white values, white culture? Why don't you dress in Western styles, eat Western foods? Why press universities to offer ethnic studies in a curriculum served perfectly well by the study of Western culture?

To many, whites and people of color alike, the questions are a sign of a new imagery. The melting pot is now an ethnic salad.

The simplistic solution is to cut ethnic roots.

"The day we can just call ourselves Americans comes after the day that we can figure out what we call each other," Olguin says. "After centuries of antagonism,

it's naive to think that we can just forget all of that."

"God, if we could all just be Americans," says Cordova. "But there is such a thing as reality, and it's borne out by the acts of the past weeks. There is racism in this country. As long as we have to call ourselves something, I'm proud to be a Filipino American. What you call yourself, hell, that's up to you."

Cecilia Concepcion Alvarez, an artist, believes the white majority and the society it dominates eye the immigrating cultures with suspicion because the country has never been racially homogenous.

Some whites fear - singly and collectively, consciously or not - giving any other culture or its people even a sliver of power. Minorities sometimes fear losing their personal identity to a nameless mass.

"We have to talk about that. We can't just dismiss it," says Alvarez. "A lot of people have been dismissed in the past. It's not cultural; it's not even necessarily genetics. It's human, and the discussion has to be how we can get together."

So how do we get together? One way is to recognize and respect each other's identity, rather than insist everyone adopt the same identity.

Nona Brazier argues that clinging to separate labels does not necessarily detract from the idea of a united people.

"One of the best things about this country is the variety," she says. "I think people need to accentuate the

American, but people also need to accentuate the love of their history and culture."

The UW's Bosmajian offers the following anecdote:

During the late 1960s, at a panel discussion on the Vietnam War, one of the panelists used the phrase "our colored boys," a phrase that Bosmajian points out is triply offensive. The phrase erected a wall that divided the participants along racial lines and blocked further communication.

"You're not going to change race relations by changing the language," Bosmajian says. "You're not going to get jobs by changing the language. But changing the language is one of the steps that has to be taken. . . . At least we'd be talking to each other." ■

---

black: The word *black* comes from Old English *blæc* ("dark") and Proto-Germanic *blakaz* ("burned"). In the 13th and 14th centuries, it came to refer to things that were deadly, malignant, foul, soiled, wicked, terrible or disastrous—the color of sin and sorrow. These negative associations were projected by the English onto the first dark-skinned people they encountered in Africa, India, and elsewhere.

Black was regarded as a slave term by African Americans who, after the Civil War, preferred *African* or *free person of color*. The term *colored* dates from earliest slave days, and *Afro American* was first recorded in 1853. Around the turn of the 19th century, *Negro* was preferred by many black people, and in the late 1960s, the epithet "black" (meaning evil, sinister, etc.) was deliberately converted by black people to a term of power and militancy, as in *Black Panthers*. In the 1970s, *black* began to give way to *Afro-American* and then, in the 1980s, to *African American*, which is preferred by many today.

white: As a reference to a racial category, the term came into use in the early 17th century, and is often equated with the old racial category *Caucasian*. In early colonial days, there was no concept of whiteness as we know that term today. The colonial British considered themselves *people*. When the term *white* emerged, it was reserved primarily for people of English ancestry, and included both cultural and physical traits. The Naturalization Law, which passed in 1790 and remained in effect until 1952, specified that naturalized citizenship was reserved for "whites." Italians, Irish, Catholics and Jews were not included, and only came to be identified as white over time. Greeks, Armenians, Lebanese, Iranians, Asian Americans and many Latin Americans have been coming under the rubric slowly.

All-American: The term *American* derives from the Italian navigator Amerigo Vespucci who explored America on voyages made between 1499 and 1504. Before the 18th century, the term was synonymous with *Indians*. People of European descent in North America were known by their nationality (English, French, etc.). As the European colonial population swelled, these immigrants and their descendants came to be known as Americans, and by the eve of the American Revolution, Native Americans and blacks were excluded from the term.

In current usage, *American* sometimes implies ethnic or racial affiliation. The terms *real American, true American, all-American,* and *100 percent American,* are often equated with white, native-born, English-speaking residents, excluding all others. These terms are sometimes used as code words, allowing speakers to conceal their prejudices by excluding immigrants and "non-whites" without specifically naming them as such.

Refs: The Color of Words: An Encyclopedic Dictionary of Ethnic Bias in the United States, Philip Herbst. Washington Models for the Evaluation of Bias Content in Instructional Materials. OSPI

Notes: _____

_____

_____

_____

_____

_____

_____

_____

_____

_____

_____

_____

_____

_____

_____

_____

_____

_____

_____

_____

_____

_____

_____

_____

_____

_____

THE POWER OF LANGUAGE

"Sticks and stones can break my bones and names can also hurt me."

© Randie Gottlieb, Ed.D.

"Dumb blonde!" "Lazy Mexican!" "Welfare queen!" Words have power. They create images in our minds. Words have been used to divide people into "us" and "them," and to reinforce stereotypes and prejudice. Some words are obviously negative—intended to cause hurt, but biased language is not always obvious. Subtle messages in our everyday vocabulary can also cause harm. Are we communicating what we intend, or inadvertently excluding others and perpetuating stereotypes? Since language both reflects and structures our thoughts, and thoughts affect our behavior, more inclusive language can build bridges, tear down walls, and help create a culture where all people feel treated with dignity and respect.

Negative Language
Name calling, ridicule, jokes, rumors, teasing, stereotypes, disrespect, put downs, silence...

- Can cause increased stress
- Decreased attention span
- Loss of motivation and self esteem
- Fear, anger, frustration
- Poor concentration in school

Positive Language
You can do it, good try, glad to see you, come join us, nice work, I believe in you...

- Can encourage and empower
- Enhance dignity and self-worth
- Increase confidence and motivation
- Improve relationships
- Increase success in school

Some Common Terms Revisited

Old perceptions can be frozen into our language and unconsciously influence us to see the world in an outmoded way. Many biased terms are so familiar that we are unaware of the discomfort they cause to others. Ending such bias takes mindfulness and practice. Review the following terms and explain why they might be considered biased or hurtful.

all-American	illegal alien	reverse racism
America	Indian giver	that's so retarded
blacklist	jewed him down	that's really gay
civilized	little white lie	the European continent
classical music	minorities	trailer trash
Dark Ages	new world	typical white male
foreign languages	no way, José	Westward movement
gay lifestyle	non-white	women's history
gypped	politically correct	World Series
how the West was won	proper English	you people

Why Are These Statements Problematic?

1. Mind if I call you George? *(to Jorge)*
2. They're acting like a bunch of wild Indians.
3. We should include the Muslims in our discussions on tolerance.
4. Mr. Rogers and Vanessa received awards for excellence in teaching.
5. She's an intelligent African American student and should go far.

Counterparts and Opposites

Words focus our attention and can subtly assign blame or promote a particular point of view, e.g., the same person can be a *rebel* or a *patriot*, a *freedom fighter* or *terrorist*—depending on who is speaking. Change the terminology and you can change the perception.

What is the difference between these terms?	
He's a stud.	She's a slut.
They were slaves.	They were enslaved.
cotton plantation	slave labor camp
pioneer or settler	colonizer or invader
culture of poverty	unjust economic system
white privilege	white domination
riot	uprising

Add your own examples below.	
old people	elders

Person-First Language

Person-first language is a more respectful way to refer to someone with an illness or disability. The person is described as **having** the disability, not **as** the disability. The focus is on capabilities rather than limitations. The use of outdated language perpetuates old stereotypes of people with disabilities as helpless burdens or tragic victims. There is much disagreement about which terms are considered offensive. For example, some say "differently abled" is now acceptable, while others feel it is an awkward and unnecessary euphemism. The goal is courtesy and respect. Here are a few examples. Add your own.

Disability First	Person First
She's wheelchair bound.	She uses a wheelchair.
He's a victim of cerebral palsy.	He has cerebral palsy.
She's a cripple.	She walks with a limp.
albinos	people with albinism
the deaf	
the retarded	
the disabled	

> **A Riddle:** A man and his son were in a car accident. They were each taken to different hospitals. When the boy was rushed into the operating room, the surgeon took one look and exclaimed, "I can't operate on that boy. He's my son!" *(Explain.)*

Gender-Biased Language

Manning the phones, showing good sportsmanship, counting man-hours, voting for chairman—this is the language of a male-centered culture. Such language is no longer accurate or appropriate. It excludes half of the human race. A linguistic double standard also reinforces sexism in our society. For the same behaviors, men are considered assertive; women are pushy. He is confident; she is stubborn. He's a bachelor; she's an old maid. Gender bias has shaped the thought patterns of both sexes for centuries. These antiquated patterns will gradually change as we learn to employ more inclusive terms in our daily speech.

Suggest gender-neutral alternatives for the following terms:

Words with "man"

caveman	_____
chairman	_____
common man	_____
family of man	_____
freshman	_____
layman	_____
man the booth	_____
man-hours	_____
mankind	_____
manmade	_____
manpower	_____
man-sized	_____
men working	_____
snowman	_____
sportsmanship	_____

Occupational Titles

anchorman	_____
congressman	_____
craftsman	_____
fireman	_____
fisherman	_____
foreman	_____
handyman	_____
housewife	_____
lady lawyer	_____
mailman	_____
male nurse	_____
newsman	_____
policeman	_____
stewardess	_____
weatherman	_____

What's the difference? ▶ governor/governess ▶ master/mistress ▶ He's/She's a professional.

What does it mean? ▶ To mother children ▶ To father children
▶ Man up ▶ Take it like a man ▶ Man-to-man talk ▶ Act like a lady

A few more: ▶ You guys ▶ forefathers ▶ gentlemen's agreement ▶ bachelor's degree
▶ Mr. and Mrs. Kevin Ono ▶ black tie dinner ▶ man and wife ▶ may the best man win

---

Ladies First? Examine the common word pairs below.

- ladies and gentlemen
- Adam and Eve
- king and queen
- Jack and Jill

- his and hers
- men and women
- boys and girls
- brothers and sisters

- Mr. and Mrs.
- husband and wife
- Romeo and Juliet
- male and female

1. What do you notice about the word order in each phrase?
2. What assumptions are inherent in usually placing males first?
3. Is there a natural order to gender relationships?
4. Now read each phrase aloud, reversing the word order.
5. Does it make a difference? Do your perceptions change?

Rewrite the following sentences:

1. Each student is expected to do his own work.
2. Ask your mothers to bring snacks to the party.
3. If you need anything, just ask the girls in the front office.
4. The reading list included Shakespeare, Hemingway, and Emily Dickinson.
5. Local realtor Alex Garcia, 47, and Sandra Day, petite 50-year-old mother of two, have entered the race.

Language is not an exact map of reality, but a label or category in our minds. It's a tool to help us reach a shared understanding of the world.

"When I use a word," Humpty Dumpty said in a rather scornful tone, "it means just what I choose it to mean—neither more nor less." "The question is," said Alice, "whether you can make words mean so many different things." "The question is," said Humpty Dumpty, "which is to be master—that is all." – Lewis Carroll, *Alice in Wonderland*

Naming and defining is a prerogative of power.

Language can also be used to maintain power by:

- Stripping others of their own languages
- Denying them access to education and literacy
- Generating rules of proper usage as a marker of class and race
- Determining which voices may speak and which are silenced
- Structuring language in such a way that it masks power

Language can be used to exaggerate, mislead, belittle, slander, inflame passions, scapegoat others, generate fear, and outright lie.

Language can reinforce inequality and legitimize privilege, for example, when women are trivialized by such terms as honey, cupcake, chick, baby, kitten, girl and doll.

Language reveals and reinforces our cultural expectations about appropriate roles. If one sex dominates a category (e.g., women in nursing), and a non-dominant person fills that position, we tend to add a marker, e.g., "male nurse" or "Black professor"—which creates the impression that the person is violating a norm.

Words can also be used to encourage and empower, to restore trust, to envision new possibilities, to tell the truth, and to heal.

Refs: Communicating Gender Diversity: A Critical Approach, by Victoria Pruin DeFrancisco & Catherine Helen Palczewski, SAGE Publications; Understanding the Power of Naming and Language, www.unesco.org; The Power of Names, Adam Alter, newyorker.com.

Culturally Responsive Teaching

© Randie Gottlieb, Ed.D.

Culturally responsive teaching (CRT) can be defined as providing inclusive bias-free curriculum and instruction, and using the cultural knowledge and experiences of diverse students to make learning more relevant and effective.

Even with the best educational practices and instructional materials, we won't reach our local, state or national academic goals without culturally responsive classrooms. Our efforts will be undermined if teachers are unaware of students' backgrounds and learning styles, or if they communicate unconscious prejudices, stereotypes and lowered expectations for certain students.

Teacher attitudes towards language and culture, along with status and power relationships in the school setting, can have a significant influence on student motivation and learning. Language is a key element of cultural identity, a carrier of cultural values and knowledge, a connection to history, to family, to systems of support. Some people believe that students need to give up their home language and culture in order to blend into American society. But children whose language and culture are positively valued, and who feel they belong in the system, are more likely to succeed academically. A student who feels anxious or unwelcome (whether due to immigrant status, racial prejudice, gender stereotypes or other reason) will find it harder to learn. Teachers can counteract this by reinforcing the idea that diversity is a strength that adds value to our world.

For some students, the attempt to bridge two worlds may result in alienation from both. They may have rejected the old culture, but are resentful at not yet being fully accepted into the new. Some students withdraw or develop an oppositional identity, resisting learning and sabotaging their own achievement. This coping strategy may help to preserve a sense of self, to protect students from further psychological assault, and to avoid rejection by their peers.

A significant factor behind the poor academic achievement of low-income and ethnic minority students, is the discontinuity between their home cultures and school. By drawing on students' linguistic strengths, and incorporating their life experiences and cultural content into the curriculum, teachers can make learning more relevant and effective, increase motivation, and build bridges between home, school and community.

Instruction is also more effective when teaching and learning styles match. Teachers can design lessons and assessments to address multiple intelligences, diverse learning styles and different ways of communicating. Good teaching is not identical for all students under all circumstances. How can we create an environment conducive to learning if we only use a single mode of instruction? And how can we differentiate instruction if we don't see differences?

Teachers can also use cooperative learning, peer teaching and other inclusive techniques to promote positive interactions among students from diverse backgrounds and encourage the development of a classroom community.

An inclusive curriculum helps students understand and interpret events and concepts from multiple perspectives. It incorporates authentic multicultural literature and the history, contributions and current experience of different genders, religious communities and ethnic groups. It utilizes videos and role models from diverse backgrounds when bringing resource people into the school. It encourages open discussion of basic diversity concepts including prejudice, stereotyping, racism, discrimination, and how to recognize and respond to different forms of bias.

Textbooks form the basis of most classroom instruction, but they often exclude or distort information about women, ethnic minorities and low-income groups. While blatant racial and gender stereotypes have mostly been eliminated, preference is still given to white males and to middle class experiences and values. Students can be taught to think critically about these materials, and teachers can include supplementary resources to make up for the "missing chapters," ensuring that the content is as complete and accurate as possible. Debunking media myths and stereotypes should also be a central feature of culturally responsive teaching.

Teacher expectations have a critical effect on student achievement. Teachers are cultural beings. Without realizing it, we carry our own culture into the classroom, along with any prejudices, assumptions and misconceptions. This affects how we think, behave, teach and relate to others. Research shows that teachers tend to have lower expectations for low-income students and students of color, and that this also affects how students see themselves, negatively impacting their motivation and performance. High expectations can help students break out of this cycle. A review of effective schools, even in high poverty and ethnic minority areas, shows they have one thing in common: high expectations for all students.

Some point to the limited number of teachers of color, and believe that achievement by students of color is contingent upon filling this need. It is true that middle-class whites make up a large majority of the U.S. teaching force and will for some time. While more teachers of color are definitely needed, reform should not wait until they can be trained and hired. It is also wrong to assume that only people of color can teach students of color or engage in CRT. All teachers need to feel comfortable with inclusive, anti-bias education.

As more diverse staff enter the profession, more students will have role models, allowing them to make a personal connection—to see their own reality reflected and validated in the school setting. A diverse staff also opens possibilities for *all* students to see from multiple perspectives, to view reality through different frames of reference—avoiding some of the blind spots of the traditional curriculum. For a balanced education, students need "mirrors" as well as "windows" on the world.

While it is understandable to blame factors such as poverty, cultural differences, limited parental involvement or lack of English proficiency for poor performance in school, other factors—increasing school segregation, widespread racial steering, low-level instruction, limited educational resources, stereotyping, discrimination and harassment from peers—may have even more significant effects. Despite these obstacles, there are specific strategies, resources and training programs available to help us raise awareness and improve our educational practice.

Culturally responsive teaching is not a choice, but an imperative. The injustices in our society and our educational systems are real and ongoing. Awareness and good intentions are not enough. We need concrete knowledge, skills, moral courage and the will to act. While teachers cannot solve all of society's problems, we can make a significant difference, and we can learn on the job. Children are our most precious resource and our investment in the future. The stakes of waiting are simply too high. ∎

Refs: Geneva Gay, Culturally Responsive Teaching, Teacher's College Press
James Banks, Multicultural Education Series, University of Washington
Emily Style, Curriculum as Window and Mirror, National SEED Project

Culturally Responsive Teaching

Discussion Questions

1. What are some significant factors in the poor academic achievement of low-income students and students of color?

2. What do teachers bring into their classrooms that they may not be aware of?

3. What is the effect of teacher expectations on student achievement?

4. What is CRT and how can it improve academic performance?

5. How can teachers respond to textbooks and media with distorted or missing information?

6. Will hiring more teachers of color solve the problem?

7. List several things teachers can do as part of CRT.

8. Share any personal stories or experiences, and any questions or comments.

Notes: _____

_____

_____

_____

_____

_____

_____

_____

_____

_____

_____

_____

_____

_____

_____

_____

_____

_____

_____

_____

_____

_____

_____

_____

Paper PowerPoint - Due Day 4

Your team has five minutes to prepare a "Paper PowerPoint" on one of the sections below. Use the markers and blank paper to create up to five "slides" using text and/or images to answer the questions. Tomorrow, your team will have 1-2 minutes to present your slides during the morning review.

Item	Day 3 Review Topics
A	• Define race, how many races are there, and how do we know? • What was the eugenics movement and what effects did it have on our educational system and on society—in the past and present?
B	• Why do we have different skin colors? • What is the "one drop rule" and how was it used?
C	• Give some examples of how society treats people differently based on race or skin color.
D	• What is "colorblindness" and although well intentioned, why is it harmful? • What *does* work to reduce prejudice?
E	• Why did Isur Danielovitch become Kirk Douglas? • Why do we label people? List some positive and some negative reasons. • Which, if any, ethnic labels should we use and why? (African American or Black, Caucasian or White, Hispanic or Latino, also Latin@ or Latinx, non-white or people of color?)
F	• Why does the Western hero ride in on a white horse and why is this significant? • Words have power. (Explain)

Note: For 5 teams, combine topics B & C. For 7 teams, split topic A. For 8 teams, split topics A & B.

Notes: _____

_____

_____

_____

_____

_____

_____

_____

_____

_____

_____

_____

_____

_____

_____

_____

_____

_____

_____

_____

_____

_____

PART IV

Equity Expectations & Achievement

Equity, Expectations & Achievement

> *"If we do not change our direction, we are likely to end up where we are headed."* --Ancient Chinese proverb

Objectives
1. Define the achievement gap.
2. Explain the effect of teacher expectations on student achievement.
3. Describe some institutional barriers to equity and achievement.
4. List some classroom strategies to increase equity and achievement.

Does a student's _____
affect academic potential?

- gender   yes   no
- ethnicity   yes   no
- economic level   yes   no
- language status   yes   no

List 5-10 adjectives to describe one or more low-achieving students:

1.
2.
3.
4.
5.
6.
7.
8.
9.
10.

Some phrases that communicate high expectations:

Resources

Data Snapshot: School Discipline, Office of Civil Rights, ocrdata.ed.gov/Downloads/CRDC-School-Discipline-Snapshot.pdf

Minority Student Achievement Network, National coalition of multiracial, suburban-urban school districts that have come together to understand and eliminate achievement/opportunity gaps that persist in their schools. < msan.wceruw.org >

Falling Further Behind: Combating Racial Discrimination in America, report by The Leadership Conference, a coalition of over 200 national organizations working for civil rights. < www.civilrightsdocs.info/pdf/reports/CERD_Report.pdf >

School to Prison Pipeline (multiple articles and videos)
< neatoday.org/category/school-to-prison-pipeline >
< www.pbs.org > menu > search > school to prison pipeline
< Google > "fact sheet, school to prison pipeline, Amurao"

The New Jim Crow: Mass Incarceration in the Age of Color-blindness, by Michelle Alexander. < newjimcrow.com >

Teaching the New Jim Crow, free curriculum for grades 9-12. < www.tolerance.org/publication/teaching-new-jim-crow >

18 Things You Should Know About Mass Incarceration, Southern Poverty Law Center slide show with statistics. < www.splcenter.org > search "18 things" >

Does a teacher's race affect which students are identified as gifted? < Google > "Emma Brown race gifted"

Detracking for Excellence and Equity, by Burris and Garrity, Association for Supervision and Curriculum Development. Free online book. < www.ascd.org > search "detracking"

 # Ability Grouping & Achievement

Despite hundreds of research studies conducted over the past century, the issue of ability grouping and tracking has been highly debated for decades. Some studies indicate that ability grouping, whether between classrooms or within classrooms, can have positive effects for high achievers and negative effects for low ones. Tracking of students fell out of favor in the late 1980s under criticism that the practice perpetuated inequality by consigning poor and minority students to permanent low-level groups. A new analysis of data from the National Assessment of Educational Progress (NAEP) shows that ability grouping has re-emerged in classrooms around the country. The following articles may shed some light on the topic.

Classroom Leveling, Tracking, and Ability Grouping
School Psychologist Jason Wright
www.wrightpsych.com/popular-topics/leveled-classrooms
Clear definitions, easy-to-read, presents both pros and cons with links.

Research Spotlight on Academic Ability Grouping
National Education Association
www.nea.org/tools/16899.htm
The NEA is opposed to "discriminatory academic tracking."

Grouping Students by Ability Regains Favor in Classroom
Vivian Yee, New York Times
www.nytimes.com > search by title
The author is in favor of "dynamic grouping" within the classroom.

Achievement Effects of Ability Grouping in Secondary Schools
Dr. Robert Slavin, Director, Center for Research & Reform in Educ., Johns Hopkins Univ.
http://rer.sagepub.com/content/60/3/471
A summary of hundreds of research studies.

Achievement & Opportunity Gaps

Achievement Gap

The achievement gap refers to the persistent disparity in educational performance between groups of students, especially groups defined by socioeconomic status, race/ethnicity and gender.

The achievement gap can be observed on standardized test scores, GPAs, dropout rates, college enrollment and completion rates, and other measures.

The Gap Persists

"The black-white gap continues to be the largest one, with black students scoring about 30 points below their white peers on both tests in 2013."

Education Week

Seniors scoring proficient or above	READING	MATH
White	47%	33%
Black	16%	7%

In 2017, National Center for Education Statistics noted that the White-Black reading gap was wider than in 1992.

Correlation & Causality

A correlation between two things does not automatically mean one causes the other.

> A may cause B.
> B may cause A.
> A and B may *both* be caused by C.
> Or the correlation may be a coincidence.

Opportunity Gap

The ways in which ethnicity, economic status, access to educational resources & quality schools, English proficiency, family situation, prejudice & other factors contribute to lowered aspirations & achievement for certain groups.

Opportunity gap refers to inputs

Achievement gap refers to outputs

If inputs are not equal or equitable, we can't expect the same level of achievement.

Segregated Schools

65 years after Brown v. Board of Education, public schools have become increasingly re-segregated.

Court orders, busing and magnet programs had limited success.

Growing Hispanic enrollment, resistance to integration, White flight & racial steering contribute to this process.

Today, most Black & Latino students (75%) attend schools with a substantial majority of low-income & "minority" children. Most White & Asian students attend largely white middle-class schools.

Unequal Funding & Resources

High-minority, high-poverty schools tend to have:

> Less money per student & larger class sizes
> Less experienced, lower-paid, out-of-field teachers
> Dangerous or outdated facilities
> Less demanding curriculum
> Higher staff turnover
> "A massive inequity in resources"

US Dept. of Ed, Educator Equity, Falling Further Behind: www.civilrights.org

© Randie Gottlieb, Ed.D.

Achievement & Opportunity Gaps

Alternatives to Tracking & Labeling

To avoid placing students into fixed low-level groups:

- Learning centers
- Peer teaching
- Level reading & math
- New groups for art & music
- Mixed groups for projects
- Individualize instruction
- Dual language programs
- ELL buddies
- Cooperative learning
- After-school tutoring
- Expand gifted programs

Discriminatory Discipline

Repeated studies show:

- Unfair discipline patterns for students of color, low-income students & those with disabilities, beginning in pre-school
- Blacks & Hispanics are disciplined most
- Regardless of age, grade level or gender
- Whether in minority or mostly-white affluent schools
- Much more likely to be referred, suspended, expelled
- Significantly harsher punishments for same offense

School to Prison Pipeline

In many low-income "hyper-segregated" schools, local police are charged with discipline. Students may be physically restrained, suspended, expelled, arrested in school, or referred to the criminal justice system—even for trivial offenses.

Across the US, 70% of students arrested in school or referred to law enforcement are Black or Latino.

This practice, referred to as the "new Jim Crow," has helped to create the world's largest prison system.

"An epidemic that is plaguing schools across the nation." (PBS)

School to Prison Pipeline

What can we do?

1. Create a code of conduct with specific consequences for violations to ensure fairness.
2. Use restorative rather than punitive practices.
3. Reconsider zero tolerance policies.
4. Collect and analyze your annual discipline stats by race, gender, ability and other factors.
5. Train staff in positive behavioral interventions.
6. Teach kids consultation and conflict resolution.
7. Limit the use of law enforcement on campus.
8. Make severe punishment a last resort.

High-Stakes Testing

Pros

- Measure student achievement & track academic progress
- Help teachers design lessons based on student needs
- Compare schools, districts, states & sub-groups
- Provide data needed to develop programs & services
- Ensure that schools are accountable

Cons

- A single test score is not a fair or valid measure
- Teaching to the test takes time away from other subjects
- Less flexibility, freedom, innovation in the classroom
- Results are used to allocate educational opportunities
- Can have a punitive effect on schools, teachers & students —especially low-income & students of color & their teachers
- Used to justify stereotyping & exclusion of minority groups

Summary

Many students feel devalued, stereotyped, labeled & marginalized by the educational system. Low income & ethnic minority students are particularly at risk for low academic achievement.

Schools can narrow the achievement gap by:

- Paying attention to race, gender, class & income.
- Becoming aware of our own biases & stereotypes.
- Changing our words & actions to communicate high expectations for all.
- Honoring the languages, cultures & experiences of our students, & using these as a springboard for learning.
- Providing opportunities for extra help when needed.
- Identifying & removing institutional barriers to success.
- Creating inclusive classrooms where all know they belong.

Institutional Barriers to Equity & Achievement

Over time, an organization may develop structures, policies and practices that favor one group to the detriment of another (e.g., old boys' network, glass ceiling). These practices become part of the institutional culture—"the way things are done around here." While this power structure is accepted as the norm and is often invisible to the dominant group, to others it presents a set of very real barriers to inclusion and achievement.

Such structures are pervasive and difficult to change. They are often perpetuated unintentionally. A system of unequal treatment based on race is known as racism. Even if individuals within an organization become more accepting of others, unless the old structures are deliberately changed, institutional racism still remains.

School systems are not exempt. Although state and national education standards are intended for all students, our educational systems have not served all students equally well. Research on our public school system reveals significant differences between the experience of students of color and their peers. The following practices have been shown to have detrimental effects on access to quality education for all.

1. Segregated schools:

2. Unequal funding and resources:

3. Tracking, sorting and labeling:

4. Differential student-teacher interactions:

5. Unconscious bias and low expectations:

6. Discriminatory discipline:

7. School-to-prison pipeline:

8. Eurocentric curriculum:

9. High stakes testing:

> An example

Loving Across the Color Line:
A White Adoptive Mother Learns About Race

Dr. Sharon Rush, civil rights lawyer & University of Florida law professor

As the White mother of an adopted Black child, Sharon Rush shares her shock and dismay as she learns, during repeated encounters with prejudice, that racism is far more devastating than most Whites can ever imagine. In one example, she describes the struggles she had with two different schools to have her daughter admitted to the gifted programs.

"One month before the end of my daughter's first year at [her new] school, I was talking with a teacher …when another woman joined us, who was introduced to me as the school's gifted teacher. I responded, 'Oh, I didn't know the school had a gifted program. That's odd that no one would mention it to me because my daughter was in the gifted program in her previous school.' …The gifted teacher warmly responded, 'Oh, if your daughter was in the gifted program at her previous school, she should definitely be in it here. I'll check her file and get right back to you.'"

Dr. Rush immediately went to her daughter's regular classroom teacher who replied, "I can understand that you are upset. We should have screened your daughter when she first joined the school. It's right in her record and we should have seen it. I can't explain why it was overlooked."

The disappointment was overwhelming because Dr. Rush had transferred her daughter to the new school precisely because of the struggle she had at the first school to get her daughter into the gifted class. That teacher and the principal placed one obstacle after another in the child's way. First there was a series of meetings with school officials in June that the mother was required to attend. Then she was told her daughter must first be tested to see if she qualified for the program. But she had already been tested and did qualify. Yet the matter was still pending by the time school started in the Fall.

Upset, Dr. Rush called the principal, who explained in a kindly manner that in order to make the switch into the gifted program, her daughter would need to be observed to see if she was emotionally ready. The mother was assured that the observation procedure wouldn't take long. By mid-October, there was still no decision. In early November, Dr. Rush called the principal again, who explained in a calm voice, "We want to make sure we don't make a mistake that could be emotionally injurious to the child."

After Dr. Rush complained to the school board, her daughter was finally admitted to the program towards the end of the Fall semester. But it was anything but a welcoming environment. She was made to feel like an alien in the gifted class. She was seated near the back where she would be less visible, and on Parent Night her presentation wasn't included with all the others, even though she had worked hard to complete her project on time. Dr. Rush knew that she needed to place her daughter in a different school.

The new school offered hope for better treatment for her daughter, but those hopes were dashed when Dr. Rush met the gifted teacher a month before school ended. Dr. Rush continues…."School officials ignored the information I gave them (in writing and orally) about my daughter's gifted placement in the prior school, they never mentioned their own gifted program to me, no one ever recommended my daughter to be evaluated for the program the entire year, and when their neglect of my daughter became evident, they cavalierly dismissed their mistake as an oversight….Is it coincidental that she was the only Black girl to successfully place into the gifted program in her grade in both schools?…These… stories about my daughter are disturbing, but they border on tragic when I stop to reflect on how hard it is for *all* Black children to beat the odds..." ∎

From Loving Across the Color Line: A White Adoptive Mother Learns About Race (chapter 3).
Pub. Rowman and Littlefield, 2000, Lanham, MD. ISBN-13:978-0847699124. Used with permission.

Once Upon a Time
in a land far, far away . . .

Imagine that you are a white student in a school system that is 95% Black. The administrators and teachers are Black. The janitors and a few classroom aides are white. Social studies, art and literature classes concentrate almost exclusively on African history, African artists and authors. Textbooks reflect the views of African American publishers and curriculum committees. The posters and photographs on the walls show the faces and artwork of Blacks. Famous quotations by Black heroes adorn each classroom.

In February, the entire school celebrates Euro-American History Day. The students learn about John F. Kennedy's assassination and march in a parade to celebrate his birthday. White students are told they are members of an ethnic minority group whose ancestors from Europe were a backward, barbaric people with a pagan religion.

When several white families moved into the district this past fall, a number of classmates transferred to a new school. Black flight to the suburbs has become commonplace. Ethnic slurs are heard more frequently as well. On a typical school day, you count 17 examples—variations on the theme of "white trash," "redneck," and "marshmallow scum."

White students are often ignored in class. When a fight breaks out or school rules are broken, whites are often sent to the principal and disciplined, while Blacks are reprimanded and excused. In fact, a recent study by the local university shows that whites are more likely to be referred, suspended or expelled than Blacks, for the same offense. Most of the white students are in special education or remedial classrooms. The few whites who advance into the upper level classes are told they are in the wrong place. Upon graduation, if they make it that far, the school counselor may suggest they forgo college, and aim for something more practical— for their own good. ∎

© Randie Gottlieb, Ed.D.

Notes: _____

_____

_____

_____

_____

_____

_____

_____

_____

_____

_____

_____

_____

_____

_____

_____

_____

_____

_____

_____

_____

_____

_____

_____

Readings on Equity, Expectations & Achievement

UnityWorks Training Institute

-1- **The Roots of Racism in American Schools** From colonial times to government policies, textbooks, scientific and religious beliefs.	-2- **Targeting Black Boys & School to Prison Pipeline** A brief outline of the "psychological genocide" taking place in our nation's schools.	-3- **Native American Learners & Checklist of Do's and Don'ts** History of Indian Education and why many Native students don't succeed in school.	-4- **Whites in Multicultural Ed: Rethinking Our Role** Privilege and the luxury of ignorance; emotions that harm and responses that heal.
-5- **The Question of Class: Beyond the Culture of Poverty** Understanding the relationships between poverty, class and education.	-6- **Effectiveness of Dual Language Education for All** A comparison of language learning programs and their impact on academic achievement.	-7- **Gender and Schooling: Some Considerations** Title IX, biased curricula, stereotypes, gender gaps and strategies for improving gender equity.	-8- **Teacher Expectations and Student Achievement** What is the relationship between expectations and achievement, and what does it mean for teachers?

1 The Roots of Racism in American Schools

Summary by Randie S. Gottlieb, Ed.D.

Based on the book, "The Racial Conditioning of Our Children" by Nathan Rutstein
National Resource Center for the Healing of Racism, Michigan, 2001

How did racism begin in American schools? The first European settlers brought it with them to our shores. Long before America existed, the ancient Greeks, led by Aristotle, taught that there were superior and inferior classes of human beings. There were those without souls and those with souls who were destined to rule over them. This idea was viewed as scientific truth, endorsed by religion and taught in the great universities of Europe.

Early European Christians believed that dark-skinned peoples carried the "Curse of Ham." According to the Bible, Noah's son Ham had seen him naked, so Noah cursed Ham's dark-skinned grandson and all his descendants. Dark skin was considered evil. Queen Elizabeth, who was obsessed with skin color, often painted her face white and tried to rid the British Isles of all blacks. Pope Nicholas V believed that blacks were soulless cannibals and that the native inhabitants of the "New World" were subhuman heathens and savages. He encouraged the clergy to enslave and sell these "beasts of burden" to fund the work of the Church.

In the colonies of the early 1600's, Puritan political and religious leaders taught that Native Americans were the agents of Satan, and that white Christians had the divine right to conquer the land they occupied and to rule over them. When the colonists fought the Indians, they believed they were waging a holy war, and that God was on their side.

This same attitude was reflected in the colonial schools, which educated only white students. Teachers and textbooks reinforced the notion that only whites were fully human, intelligent, creative, civilized and worthy of leadership. According to the texts, all the inventors, explorers, authors, artists, builders, political leaders and war heroes had light skin. Uncle Sam, a leading symbol of America, was a white man.

The Encyclopedia Britannica, in its first edition in 1798, described the Negro as a people of "idleness, treachery, revenge, cruelty, impudence, stealing, lying, debauchery, nastiness and intemperance… and an awful example of the corruption of man." In its 11th edition in 1911, the Britannica asserted that "the Negro would appear to stand on a lower evolutionary plane than the white man."[1] While it is true that this was published almost 100 years ago, the people who read and believed that assessment, passed the same message along to their children. Added to other bits of misinformation proclaimed by America's leading politicians and religious leaders, this continual brainwashing was absorbed as truth, and passed down generation after generation up to the present day.

This distorted view of humanity soon became incorporated into the laws of the country. For example, in 1789, the Massachusetts legislature made it against the law to teach reading and writing to Native Americans. The penalty for breaking the law was death. It was also illegal to educate slaves, whose destiny was to serve white society. Slave breeding became a $150 million-per-year industry in the South in the mid-1800's, and the supply of cheap labor made many whites rich. In the U.S. Constitution, our Founding Fathers decreed that a slave was to be counted as 3/5 of a human being.

Many of our nation's presidents and other prominent Americans held to the view of white superiority and black inferiority. George Washington, James Madison, Benjamin Franklin, Thomas Jefferson: these were not inherently evil men. Their attitudes were a reflection of generations of racial conditioning. Even Abraham Lincoln, before becoming president, declared in a public debate that, "I as much as any other man am in favor of the superior position being assigned to the White race." [2] Anyone who questioned white superiority or who claimed that other groups were equal to whites, was considered a lunatic.

White churches taught that race mixing was a sin. Best-selling novelist and preacher, Thomas Dixon, wrote in 1902, "One drop of Negro blood makes a Negro. It kinks the hair, flattens the nose, thickens the lips [and] puts out the light of intellect…Every inch in the approach of these races across the barriers that separate them is a movement toward death. You cannot seek the Negro vote without asking him to your home sooner or later. If you ask him to your house, he will break bread with you at last. And if you seat him at your table, he has the right to ask your daughter's hand in marriage." [3]

Although granted citizenship after the Civil War, blacks were prevented from voting and owning property by organizations like the Klan. And although the Civil Rights laws of the 1960's desegregated public water fountains, "they couldn't remove the suspicion, anger, rage, fear, anxiety, hatred, frustration and feelings of superiority and inferiority from the hearts of those lined up in the integrated queue. No law can eliminate the effects of 400 years of racial conditioning." [4]

Modern "scientific" racism was born in 1735, with the publication of a work by Swedish biologist, Carlos Von Linneaus, who had developed a system for classifying all living things. He grouped humans into four categories:

1. Americanus: reddish with straight black hair, quick-tempered, paints himself with fine red lines
2. Asiaticus: sallow with black hair, dark eyes, melancholy, stiff, haughty and avaricious
3. Africanus: black with frizzled black hair, flat nose, thick lips, sluggish, crafty, indolent
4. Europeaus: white with long flowing hair, blue eyes, muscular, gentle, cheerful, inventive

Linneaus' fractured view of humanity was hailed as a major scientific breakthrough, and with the advent of the printing press, was distributed throughout Europe and North America. This concept of the separate races of man became the basis for university biology curricula and was incorporated in teacher education programs throughout the country. Building on Linneaus' work, future scientists ranked the races, putting Africans on the bottom and Caucasians on the top. They reasoned that Jesus Christ was white and the Son of God, therefore whites most resembled God since humans were created in His image.

In the 1840's, the American physician Dr. Josiah Nott measured the heads of blacks and whites, concluding "scientifically" that blacks generally had smaller heads, and therefore smaller brains, making them less intelligent. University biology courses incorporated Nott's erroneous findings.

In 1995, the world's leading geneticists and biologists gathered in Austria to assess the validity of the concept of race. They concluded that, "the nineteenth-century notion of races as discreet and different entities is false. There is only gradual genetic diversity between groups…Nearly all the physically observable differences reflect very limited total adaptations to climate and other specific environmental conditions." [5] In other words, there is only one human race. While current genetic research has abundantly confirmed this fact, most people still believe in the idea of separate races, some superior to others.

This belief forms the core of our modern academic curriculum. When today's students learn mainly about authors, artists, composers and kings with Anglo-Saxon names, the myth of racial superiority is perpetuated. When textbooks teach that Columbus discovered America, it implies that the native peoples who were here first, didn't really matter. When a history course on World Civilizations omits the cultures of Africa, Asia and pre-Columbian North and South America, it reinforces the idea that only whites contributed to the development of civilization, and makes people of color feel excluded and insignificant. When an English literature class reads only white authors, racism continues to silently poison the minds of America's schoolchildren, no matter what the color of their skin. ∎

Refs: 1-5. Rutstein, pgs. 88, 102, 94, 89 and 131 respectively

2) Targeting Black Boys for Failure
by Randie Gottlieb, based on an essay in The Best of Emerge Magazine, p. 55-59

In his insightful essay, "Targeting Black Boys for Failure," Lee Daniels argues that school systems are targeting Black boys for failure by labeling them at an early age as troublemakers, slow learners and discipline problems. This labeling provides the rationale for disproportionately assigning them to special education, vocational classes and other "tracks of least opportunity," and all too often, completely derails their chances for future academic success.

Saddled with the stereotype that Black males are inherently dangerous and must be controlled, they are subjected to discriminatory discipline practices and "siphoned off into an educational netherworld in which the incentive to drop out increases with each year in school." Having dropped out, they face long-term unemployment or underemployment, and become vulnerable to irresponsible or even criminal behavior.

"The school-certified transformation of a Black boy from boisterous child to troublemaker often is imposed quickly and with chilling finality." For many Black boys, especially those in high-poverty inner-city neighborhoods, proper middle-class school culture stands in sharp contrast to the aggressive behavior and fighting skills needed at home to survive.

Once labeled, Black boys become "ensnared in a vicious circular trap." It becomes clear to them that teachers think they are not smart or good, and classmates insult them for being dumb. Faced with such low expectations, they begin to think of themselves as inferior. Angry at being labeled, feared and despised, they often do become troublemakers. Continued misbehavior at least brings some attention. "They intuitively know that if they were quiet and good, no one would pay any attention to them at all." ■

I Could See Myself as a Slave
by John Joyce, former Dean of Students of a school district in New York State,
from The Racial Conditioning of Our Children by Nathan Rutstein. Used with permission.

…Englewood had four elementary schools, two junior high schools and one high school. One school was all Black, appropriately named after Abraham Lincoln. Those who attended Lincoln didn't have contact with White students until they entered high school.

I guess I was considered fortunate because I attended a school that was 97% White. I don't remember much of my years in school. Maybe it is my way of blocking out the experience. But when I dig deep and recall what I endured in school I'm seized by a sense of sorrow, inner pain and anger. I remember feeling dumb in relationship to the student body. I felt like I didn't belong.

I experienced academic difficulties early on… I had to repeat the second and fifth grades. Because I felt uneasy, unwanted, I often skipped school. While in class, which was sheer torture, I felt confused. There were times when I understood the material, but when it came time to share what I knew in class, I was too inhibited to express myself clearly. Those were agonizing moments. My White classmates always seemed to know what was being asked and how to give the required answers. This was true in all subjects except gym, where I was always among the best in class.

Although I did not do well academically and missed a lot of school, I don't remember any of my teachers or a counselor or the principal sitting down with me to figure out what was happening to me. It was as if I didn't count. Everything in the school reflected White superiority. I saw people like myself reflected nowhere in the cultural fabric of the school or the materials we studied from— that is, until it came time to study slavery. Then I could see myself as a slave.

I can remember early on developing feelings of inferiority, thinking that all White kids were smart and all Black kids were dumb. The only way I could feel smart was to think that I was smarter than the other Black kids in school. So, the Black kids learned to put each other down. And this was done a lot. We called each other stupid, laughed at each other when we made a mistake or got low grades on tests…It was our way of gaining some self-esteem. The fact that the teachers and principal did nothing to stop the put downs was another indication to me that we Black kids didn't count.

When our put downs led to schoolyard fights, we finally gained some recognition and respect from the White kids. I must confess, I gained pleasure in staring down a White kid and seeing him quiver. To uphold the respect we had gained, we put a lot more effort into excelling in gym and sharpening our fighting skills than in our academic work. I think if I would have had a strong African American role model in school, I would have gotten a lot more out of school than learning how to use my fists in order to gain some respect. ■

The School-to-Prison Pipeline
Summary by Randie Gottlieb, references below

The practice of pushing students—especially students of color—out of school and into the juvenile and criminal justice systems has become known as the "school-to-prison pipeline." A 2014 Dept. of Education study[1] found that the public school suspension rate among Black students is almost three times that for Whites, with 20% of Black boys receiving an out-of-school suspension. Moreover, while Black students make up 16% of enrollments, they represent 27% of those referred to law enforcement and 31% of those who are arrested at school. A Black boy born in 2001 has a 1 in 3 chance of going to prison in his lifetime.[2,3]

A wealth of research over the past two decades indicates that Black students do *not* act out more frequently than their White counterparts, however, they *are* more likely to be referred, suspended or expelled for the same offense. Many schools in high-poverty areas rely on police rather than educators to maintain discipline. School Resource Officers patrol the halls, "often with little or no training in working with youth. As a result, students are far more likely to be subject to school-based arrests—the majority of which are for non-violent offenses…"[4] In New York City, for example, the police department employs over 5,000 School Safety Agents, compared to only 3,000 guidance counselors in the city's schools.[2] With zero tolerance policies in place, even minor infractions such as swearing, talking back to a teacher, using a cell phone in class, or bringing a nail scissors to school, have resulted in overly-harsh punishments—regardless of the circumstances.

Being suspended from school can be life altering. It is the primary predictor for dropping out—which greatly increases the likelihood of unemployment and eventual imprisonment, "funneling millions of poor people of color, especially males, into dead end, powerless and hopeless lives." In fact, "there are more adult African Americans under correctional control today than were enslaved in 1850, a decade before the Civil War began."[5]

This mass incarceration is part of a larger system of racialized social control and permanent marginalization known as *the new Jim Crow*. "Unlike the old Jim Crow…the *Whites Only* signs are gone, and it's easy to be lulled into a belief that some people are at the bottom simply because they don't work hard or are prone to crime."[3] But the stark racial disparities in school discipline suggest otherwise, and are too large and longstanding to have occurred by chance. ■

1. http://ocrdata.ed.gov/Downloads/CRDC-School-Discipline-Snapshot.pdf
2. Falling Further Behind, 2014 report by The Leadership Conference, www.civilrights.org
3. The New Jim Crow, by Michelle Alexander, newjimcrow.com
4. www.aclu.org/fact-sheet/what-school-prison-pipeline
5. www.childrensdefense.org > "cradle prison pipeline"

Reading and the Native American Learner

From a 90-page research report by the Center for Educational Improvement, Evergreen State College & Dept. of Native Education, Office of the Superintendent of Public Instruction (OSPI). Used with permission.

American Indian students have the highest high school dropout rate of any minority group. Current research suggests that the relatively low level of academic success among these students is largely the result of discontinuities between the cultures and languages of the students' homes and communities and the language and culture of mainstream classrooms. American Indian students…are likely to view learning much of what is necessary to succeed academically (such as the standard language and the standard behavior practices of the school) as detrimental to their own language, culture and identity.

It is suggested that involuntary minority groups (those brought into American society through colonization, conquest or slavery) tend to interpret the social, economic and political barriers they face in the United States as permanent and institutionalized discrimination perpetuated against them by… dominant-group-controlled institutions such as schools. Consequently, although members of involuntary minority groups frequently emphasize the importance of education…, this verbal endorsement often belies a serious educational commitment because they view education as providing few extrinsic rewards (such as future employment opportunities) since the societal barriers they face are perceived as intractable.

In addition, American Indians and other involuntary minorities tend to respond to discriminatory treatment by the dominant group by developing an oppositional identity, where their own cultural and language differences are considered symbols of group identity that should be maintained. (These symbols support a sense of collective identity…and help the group cope under conditions of subordination.) Oppositional identities negatively influence school success because…the standard language and… behavior practices of the school…may be seen as the cultural traits of their "oppressors"…which in turn leads to resistance (whether conscious or unconscious) or ambivalence toward school learning. Among adolescents, resistance may also result from student perceptions that their teachers do not care about them.

To appreciate the educational issues currently faced by American Indians, one must first have some understanding of the history of the U.S. government's role in American Indian education. This history strongly influences the perceptions of many American Indians toward schools today.

…Under the federal policy of American Indian removal, eastern tribes were to be relocated to the "Great American Desert," which, it was thought, would never be desirable for white settlement. However, although these tribes were moved to areas that were promised to them in perpetuity, continued U.S. expansion soon negated these agreements. Many tribes…were forced to move even farther west. With the discovery of gold in California in 1848, the removal policy became an increasingly untenable option for dealing with the "Indian problem." In response, the federal government called for the assimilation of American Indians into mainstream American culture.

…Through schools it was hoped that American Indians could be stripped of their native languages and cultures, induced to learn English, and adopt the white man's religion and way of life. By 1887, more than 200 "Indian schools" had been established under federal supervision, with an enrollment of over 14,000 American Indian students. These students were severely punished if they spoke their native language or practiced their tribal traditions. Indian children were routinely forcibly removed from their families to be placed in these boarding schools.

American Indians and their communities are still dealing with these long-lasting and profoundly negative influences. Many children who spent their formative years in boarding schools grew up unable to fit comfortably into either Indian or non-Indian society. They had essentially lost their parents and the chance of a normal family life. They had been subjected to rigorous discipline combined with attacks on their personal and cultural identity. They were delayed in their social and emotional development. A large number developed severe problems in adulthood, such as alcoholism, depression and violent behavior…, and were often unprepared to provide their own children with nurturing they had not received themselves. This resulted in an upsurge in child neglect and a cycle of removal of successive generations of Indian children from their parents. ■

Teaching about Native American Issues

Adapted from: A Checklist of Dos and Don'ts*

www.understandingprejudice.org/teach/native.htm. Used with permission.

Many U.S. teachers discuss Native American history and culture, especially at Thanksgiving time. Unfortunately, the portrayal of Native Americans is often stereotypical, inaccurate and outdated. This page offers several tips on how to teach these topics more accurately and effectively.

	✗ DO NOT	✓ DO
1	Do not equate Indians with things. For example, if alphabet cards say, "A is for apple, B is for ball, I is for Indian," pick a different word so that Native peoples are not presented as objects.	Highlight the Native American philosophy of respect for every form of life and for living in harmony with nature.
2	Do not speak of Native Americans only in the past tense. There are over six million Native peoples in the U.S. today, yet many books and videos still have titles such as "How the Indians Lived."	Discuss a variety of Indian nations, such as Hopi, Lakota, and Navajo, rather than lumping all Native Americans together. Explain that each nation has its own name, language, and culture.
3	Do not perpetuate the myth that a few Europeans defeated thousands of Indians in battle. Historians say the number killed in battle was relatively small. What really defeated them were European diseases from which they had no immunity.	Challenge the stereotypes of Native Americans, and help children understand that Native Americans were no more savage than others who fought to defend their homes and communities from outside invaders.
4	Do not let children imitate Indians with stereotypes like one-word sentences (Ugh, How), Hollywood-style grammar (Me heap big hungry), or gestures (war whoops, tomahawk chops).	Understand that Native American children sometimes know more about "TV Indians" than about their own heritage, and they should not be singled out to provide "a Native perspective."
5	Do not encourage children to dress up as Indians for Halloween. Even when well intentioned, costumes involving imitation feathers, face paint, headdresses, and buckskin are disrespectful of traditional Native dress—which many would consider honorable or even sacred. Also, do not expect Native Americans to look like Hollywood movie "Indians." Native peoples come from different nations with different body structures and physical features. Many have some non-native ancestors, and none have red skin.	Choose your words carefully. Two words that often give offense in the classroom are *chief* and *squaw*. In traditional culture, chiefs are revered and Native people would never say things like "How's it going, chief?" or "We have too many chiefs, not enough Indians." Squaw was once an Algonquin word meaning "woman" but is now a disrespectful slang term. Teachers should also eliminate phrases that invoke stereotypes, such as: • You're acting like a bunch of wild Indians. • Please sit Indian-style. • Don't be an Indian giver.
6	Do not divide Indians and non-Indians into "us" and "them." Instead, explain that Indians were the first Americans and that Indians today are American citizens with the same rights as all Americans. This land has always been their home. By treaty rights, many Native peoples own their own land and are separate nations within a nation.	Teach respect. Native peoples have been treated disrespectfully for so many centuries that it is sometimes hard to recognize when they are being demeaned. Indians are people in today's world. Some of your students may have Indian ancestry. Seek to learn about Native issues so your teaching is sensitive to the needs of all students.

* Note: This checklist is based in part on materials developed by Native Nevada Classroom, the Council on Interracial Books for Children, and Wendy Rivilis. It has been excerpted, reformatted and numbered, with additional details taken from "Native Americans: What Not to Teach" by June Sark Heinrich. For more, visit www.understandingprejudice.org/readroom. This site offers a Native IQ Test— an interactive 10-item quiz which may be of interest to older students.

Rethinking Our Role

by Gary Howard, www.ghequityinstitute.com. Used with permission.

My family is not atypical among white Americans….When we open ourselves to learning about the historical perspectives and cultural experiences of other races in America, much of what we discover is incompatible with our image of a free and democratic nation….Our collective security and position of economic and political dominance have been fueled in large measure by the exploitation of other people.

The physical and cultural genocide perpetrated against American Indians, the enslavement of African peoples, the exploitation of Mexicans and Asians as sources of cheap labor—on such acts of inhumanity rests the success of the European enterprise in America. This cognitive dissonance is not dealt with easily. We can try to be aware. We can try to be sensitive. We can try to deal with the racism in our own families, yet the tension remains…

THE LUXURY OF IGNORANCE

Given the difficulty of dealing with such cognitive dissonance, it is no mystery why many white Americans simply choose to remain unaware. In fact, the possibility of remaining ignorant of other cultures is a luxury uniquely available to members of any dominant group. Throughout most of our history, there has been no reason why white Americans, for their own survival or success, have needed to be sensitive to the cultural perspectives of other groups. This is not a luxury available to people of color. If you are black, Indian, Hispanic, or Asian in the United States, daily survival depends on knowledge of white America. You need to know the realities that confront you in the workplace, in dealing with government agencies, in relation to official authorities like the police. To be successful in mainstream institutions, people of color in the U.S. need to be bicultural—able to play by the rules of their own cultural community and able to play the game according to the rules established by the dominant culture. For most white Americans on the other hand, there is only one game, and they have traditionally been on the winning team.

The privilege that comes with being a member of the dominant group, however, is invisible to most white Americans….Such privileged treatment is so much a part of the fabric of our daily existence that it escapes the conscious awareness…

EMOTIONS THAT KILL

The most prevalent strategy that white Americans adopt to deal with the grim realities of history is denial….Another response is hostility…a revival of hate crimes…overt racism… fear…a collective sense of complicity, shame or guilt. On a rational level, of course, we can say that we didn't contribute to the pain. We weren't there. We would never do such things to anyone. Yet, on an emotional level, there is a sense that we were involved somehow.

And our membership in the dominant culture keeps us connected to the wrongs, because we continue to reap the benefits of past oppression.

…Ultimately, however, guilt must be overcome, along with the other negative responses to diversity—for it, too, drains the lifeblood of our people. If we are finally to become one nation of many cultures, then we need to find a path out of the debilitating cycle of blame and guilt that has occupied so much of our national energy.

RESPONSES THAT HEAL

How do we as white Americans move beyond these negative responses to diversity and find a place of authentic engagement and positive contribution? The first step is to approach the past and the present with a new sense of honesty. Facing reality is the beginning of liberation. As white Americans we can face honestly the fact that we have benefited from racism. The point is simply to face the reality of our own privilege. We can also become supportive of new historical research aimed at providing a more inclusive and multidimensional view of our nation's past…

Along with this honesty must come a healthy portion of humility. It is not helpful for white Americans to be marching out in front with all the answers for other groups. The future belongs to those who are able to walk and work beside people of many different cultures, lifestyles and perspectives…

Honesty and humility are based on respect. One of the greatest contributions white Americans can make to cultural understanding is simply to learn the power of respect. In Spanish, the term *respeto* has a deep connotation. It goes far beyond mere tolerance or even acceptance. *Respeto* acknowledges the full humanness of other people, their right to be who they are, their right to be treated in a good way. When white Americans learn to approach people of different cultures with this kind of deep respect, our own world becomes larger and our embrace of reality is made broader and richer…

But all of this is not enough. As members of the majority population, we are called to provide more than honesty, humility and respect. The race issue for white Americans is ultimately a question of action: What are we going to do about it? It is not a black problem or an Indian problem or an Asian problem or a Hispanic problem—or even a white problem. The issue of racism and cultural diversity in the U.S. is a human problem, a struggle we are all in together. It cannot be solved by any one group. We have become embedded in the problem together, and we will have to deal with it together.

This brings us to the issue of co-responsibility. The way for us to overcome the denial, hostility, fear and guilt of the past and present is to become active participants in the creation of a better future. The healing path requires all of us to join our efforts, resources, energy and commitment. No one group can do it alone. Together we are co-responsible for the creation of a new America. ∎

⑤ The Question of Class

by Paul C. Gorski, George Mason University, www.edchange.org. Used with permission.

For too long, educators' approach to understanding the relationships between poverty, class and education has been framed by studying the behaviors and cultures of poor students and their families. If only we—in the middle and upper-middle classes—can understand *their* culture, why *those people* don't value education, why *those parents* don't attend our functions and meetings, why *those kids* are so unmotivated, perhaps we can "save" some of our economically disadvantaged students from the bleak futures before them. And so we set about studying what [some] describe as the "culture of poverty," how poor people see and experience the world, how they relate to food, money, relationships, education and other aspects of life. This, despite that research has shown again and again that no such culture of poverty exists.

It's all too easy, for even the most well-meaning of us, to help perpetuate classism by buying into that mindset, implementing activities and strategies for "working with parents in poverty" or "teaching students in poverty" that, however subtly, suggest we must fix poor people instead of eliminating the inequities that oppress them.

The question, of course, for any educator of privilege committed to educational equity is this: Do we choose to study supposed cultures or mindsets of poverty because doing so doesn't require an examination of our own class-based prejudices? By avoiding that question, we also avoid the messy, painful work of analyzing how classism pervades our classrooms and schools, never moving forward toward an authentic understanding of poverty, class and education.

What does it mean, for example, that high-poverty schools have more teachers teaching outside their areas of certification, larger numbers of teacher vacancies, and fewer experienced teachers than low-poverty schools? That they're more likely to lack full access to computers and the Internet? That they have inadequate facilities and classroom materials? Or that students in high-poverty schools are more likely than their wealthier counterparts to be subjected to overcrowded classrooms, dirty or inoperative bathrooms, less rigorous curricula and encounters with vermin such as rats and cockroaches? Or that these students are more likely to attend schools with serious teacher turnover problems and lower teacher salaries than students at low-poverty schools? And why do..."experts" on poverty so often fail to mention these inequalities?

…The reality gets worse. Children from economically disadvantaged families are more likely than their middle class or wealthy peers to suffer preventable illnesses caused by inadequate healthcare, lack of health insurance and contaminated living spaces. They're more likely to experience hunger and homelessness, to go without meals, without shelter and warmth. They're more likely to live in neighborhoods with unsafe levels of environmental pollutants, to lack safe places to play, safe water to drink, safe air to breathe.

Regardless of whether a child living in poverty wants to learn, regardless of whether she's determined to make the best life for herself, she must first overcome enormous barriers to life's basic needs—the kinds of needs that middle-class people, including most professional educators, usually take for granted: access to healthcare; sufficient food and lodging; reasonably safe living conditions. Again, none of these conditions speaks to the values or desires of students in poverty, although they may speak to the values of a nation that can afford to eliminate these inequities but chooses not to.

So where do we start? What new understandings are at the heart of the anti-classist solution in our classrooms and schools?

First, whenever somebody refers to education as the great equalizer, we must remember the injustices listed above…We must recognize, too, that people living in poverty are fully aware of these discrepancies. Second, we must recognize that students and parents from poverty simply do not have the same access to material resources that their economically advantaged peers—and many of us—take for granted.

…So let's begin to ask new questions—about ourselves: On what assumptions do we base our planning and scheduling for parent-teacher conferences? Do we assume all parents have convenient transportation, that they can afford taxi or bus fare if necessary? Do we take into account that due to a lack of living-wage jobs, many poor people must work two, three, even four jobs just to pay rent and put food on the table? Do we understand that many of these parents don't have paid leave time to attend these events? Do we consider that many parents in poverty can't afford childcare or other services necessary for their attendance?

Third, we must develop anti-classist plans of action, plans that reshape school and classroom practices to counter class inequities and injustices…On an individual level, it means transforming our consciousness and practice…We can:

- Assign work requiring computer and Internet access or other costly resources only when we can provide in-school time and materials for such work to be completed;
- Work with our schools to make parent involvement affordable and convenient by providing transportation, on-site childcare and time flexibility;
- Give students from poverty access to the same high-level curricular and pedagogical opportunities and high expectations as their wealthy peers;
- Teach about classism, consumer culture, the dissolution of labor unions, environmental pollution and other injustices disproportionately affecting the poor, preparing new generations of students to make a more equitable world;
- Keep stocks of school supplies, snacks, clothes and other basic necessities handy for students who may need them, but find quiet ways to distribute these resources to avoid singling anyone out;
- Develop curricula that are relevant and meaningful to our students' lives and draw on their experiences and surroundings;
- Fight to get our students into gifted and talented programs and to give them other opportunities usually reserved for economically advantaged students and to keep them from being assigned unjustly to special education;
- Continue to reach out to parents even when we feel they are being unresponsive; this is one way to establish trust;
- Challenge our colleagues when they stigmatize poor students and their parents, reminding them of the inequitable conditions in our schools and classrooms; and
- Challenge ourselves, our biases and prejudices, by educating ourselves about the cycle of poverty and classism in and out of U.S. schools.

Most importantly, we should never, under any circumstance, make an assumption about a student or parent—about their values or culture or mindset—based on a single dimension of their identity. There is no more a single culture of poverty than there is a single culture of woman-ness or of African American-ness. And yet, some of us who would be immediately critical of a book or workshop on how to teach to *all* women or *all* African Americans—as if all women or African Americans learn in the same way—tend to apply such a narrow lens when it comes to economically disadvantaged students.

The truth is, the "culture of poverty" is a myth. What does exist is a culture of classism, a culture most devastating to our most underserved students. And *this* is a culture worth changing. ■

Drs. Virginia Collier & Wayne Thomas, George Mason University, NABE Journal of Research and Practice, www.thomasandcollier.com/professional-journal-articles.html. Used with permission.

Abstract

Our longitudinal research findings from one-way and two-way dual language enrichment models of schooling demonstrate the substantial power of this program for enhancing student outcomes and **fully closing the achievement gap** in second language (L2) students. Effect sizes for dual language are very large compared to other programs for English learners (ELLs). Dual language schooling also can transform the experience of teachers, administrators and parents into an inclusive and supportive school community for all. Our research findings of the past 18 years are summarized here, with focus on ELLs' outcomes in one-way and two-way, 50:50 and 90:10, dual language models, including heritage language programs for students of bilingual and bicultural ancestry who are more proficient in English than in their heritage language.

Key Concepts

This is not just a research report, this is a wakeup call to the field of bilingual education, written for both researchers and practitioners. We use the word *astounding* in the title because we have been truly amazed at the elevated student outcomes resulting from participation in dual language programs. Each data set is like a mystery because you never know how it's all going to turn out when you start organizing a school district's data files for analyses. But, after almost two decades of program evaluation research that we have conducted in 23 large and small school districts from 15 different states, representing all regions of the U.S. in urban, suburban and rural contexts, we continue to be astonished at the power of this school reform model.

The Pertinent Distinction: Enrichment vs. Remediation

Enrichment dual language schooling closes the academic achievement gap in L2 and in first language (L1) students initially below grade level, and for all categories of students participating in this program. **This is the only program for English learners that fully closes the gap.** In contrast, remedial models only partially close the gap. Once students leave a special remedial program and join the curricular mainstream, we find that, at best, they make one year's progress each school year (just as typical native English speakers do), thus maintaining but not further closing the gap. Often, the gap widens again as students move into the cognitive challenge of the secondary years where former ELLs begin to make less than one year's progress per year.

We classify all of the following as remedial programs: intensive English classes (such as those proposed in the English-only referenda in California, Arizona and Massachusetts), English as a second language (ESL) pullout, ESL content/sheltered instruction (when taught as a program with no primary language support), structured English immersion, and transitional bilingual education. These remedial programs may provide ELLs with very important support for one to four years. But, we have found that even four years is not enough time to fully close the gap. Furthermore, if students are isolated from the curricular mainstream for many years, they are likely to lose ground to those in the instructional mainstream, who are constantly pushing ahead. To catch up to their peers, students below grade level must make more than one year's progress every year to eventually close the gap.

In contrast to remedial programs that offer "watered down" instruction in a "special" curriculum focused on one small step at a time, dual language enrichment models are the curricular mainstream taught through two languages. Teachers in these bilingual classes create the cognitive challenge through thematic units of the core academic curriculum, focused on real-world problem solving that stimulate students to make more than one year's progress every year, in both languages. **With no translation and no repeated lessons in the other language, separation of the two languages is a key component of this model.** Peer teaching and teachers using cooperative learning strategies to capitalize on this effect serve as an important stimulus for the cognitive challenge. Both one-way and two-way enrichment bilingual programs have this power.

Differences in One-way and Two-way Dual Language Education

One-way: We define one-way programs as demographic contexts where only one language group is being schooled through their two languages. For example, along the U.S.-Mexican border, many school districts enroll students mainly of Hispanic-American heritage. Some students are proficient in English, having lost their heritage language. Others are very proficient in Spanish and just beginning to learn English. Whatever mix of English and Spanish proficiency is present among the student population, an enrichment dual language program brings these students together to teach each other the curriculum through their two heritage languages. Similar sociolinguistic situations are present along the U.S.-Canadian border for students of Franco-American heritage. Other examples of demographic contexts for one-way dual language programs can be found among American Indian schools working on native language revitalization, as well as in urban linguistic enclaves where very few native English speakers enroll in inner city schools.

Implementers of one-way programs must make their curricular decisions to meet the needs of their student population, so the resulting program design can be quite different from that of a two-way program. But, the basic principles are the same—a minimum of six years of bilingual instruction (with eight years preferable for full gap closure in L2 when there are no English-speaking peers enrolled in the bilingual classes), separation of the two languages of instruction, focus on the core academic curriculum rather than a watered-down version, high cognitive demand of grade-level lessons, and collaborative learning in engaging and challenging academic content across the curriculum.

Two-way: Two-way programs have the demographics to invite native English-speaking students to join their bilingual and ELL peers in an integrated bilingual classroom. Two-way classes can and should include all students who wish to enroll, including those who have lost their heritage language and speak only English. These bilingual classes do not need to enroll exactly 50% of each linguistic group to be classified as two-way, but it helps the process of L2 acquisition to have an approximate balance of students of each language background. For our data analyses, we have chosen a ratio of 70:30 as the minimum balance required to have enough L2 peers in a class to stimulate the natural second language acquisition process.

In addition to enhanced second language acquisition, two-way bilingual classes resolve some of the persistent sociocultural concerns that have resulted from segregated transitional bilingual classes. Often, negative perceptions have developed with classmates assuming that those students assigned to the transitional bilingual classes were those with "problems," resulting in social distance or discrimination and prejudice expressed toward linguistically and culturally diverse students enrolled in bilingual classes. Two-way bilingual classes taught by sensitive teachers can lead to a context where students from each language group learn to respect their fellow students as valued partners in the learning process with much knowledge to teach each other. ■

(7) Gender and Schooling

© Randie Gottlieb, Ed.D.

In 1972, Title IX, which prohibits sex discrimination in education, became federal law. Before Title IX, high schools typically segregated certain classes by sex. For example, boys took shop and were encouraged to study math and science; girls were required to take home economics. Only 7.4% of all high school athletes were girls, compared with 42% in 2011.[1]

Twenty years later, in 1992, the American Association of University Women sponsored a study on the academic achievement gap between girls and boys. The study documented that teachers gave girls far less attention; that textbooks reinforced gender stereotypes; and that females were subjected to widespread sexual harassment in schools. It presented "compelling evidence that girls are not receiving the same quality or even quantity, of education as their brothers" and concluded that "shortchanging girls—the women of tomorrow—shortchanges America."[2]

Today, the gender gap has narrowed. While still underrepresented in upper-level STEM courses including computer technology, female enrollment in math and science courses has dramatically increased. Girls often outpace boys in reading and writing, they tend to get better grades overall, and the gap in college enrollments has reversed. Girls are catching up on many negative behaviors as well, including smoking, drinking, bullying and early sexual activity. They are also troubled by a higher incidence of depression, low self-esteem and serious eating disorders.

Boys face their own challenges. They are far more likely to have reading difficulties, to be disciplined more harshly for the same offense, to be referred to special education, to be labeled with ADHD and prescribed Ritalin or other drugs, to be suspended and expelled, and to drop out of school.[3] Boys are also the targets of sexual harassment, usually in the form of insults challenging their masculinity, or social pressure to conform to traditional career choices and "appropriate" gender roles.

Some educators reason that with fewer male teachers at the elementary level, students come to believe that education is for girls. Good behavior may be seen as a feminine trait, and female teachers may relate better to female students, who have learning and communication styles that are similar to their own. While good teaching is not dependent on gender, the scarcity of men in K-12 classrooms sends a silent message about male and female roles.

With regard to the curriculum, although some progress has been made over the years, text books and lesson plans still minimize the experiences and contributions of women. And despite a higher percentage of females enrolled in college, subtle and not-so-subtle cultural cues tend to channel males and females into different career paths (physics, engineering and computer science vs. nursing, social work and child care), with different paychecks and levels of influence—reflecting biases of the wider society. As of June 2019, for example, only 33 of the Fortune 500 companies (6.6%) were headed by female CEOs, and a record high of 25 out of 100 seats in the U.S. Senate were held by women.[4]

Regardless of how either gender is currently performing in school, the fact remains that neither may be reaching their full potential, and that deep-seated gender stereotypes and prejudices, which hurt all children, are still strong.

Some strategies for improving gender equity at school include:

Campus Climate
- Discipline students fairly and not based on male or female behavioral stereotypes.
- Adopt a clear written policy that defines and prohibits sexual harassment and discrimination.
- Communicate the policy and specify procedures for reporting violations.
- Investigate complaints promptly, protect whistleblowers against retaliation, and take corrective action.
- Provide opportunities for students to openly discuss bullying, harassment and discrimination based on sex, gender identity or sexual orientation, and to consider ways to create a more inclusive campus environment.
- Create mentoring programs that involve more men in schools, especially at the elementary level.

Teacher Expectations and Behaviors
- Maintain high expectations for both girls and boys in all subjects.
- Develop a system for dividing attention fairly among all students.
- Move around the room to be physically near all students.
- Allow more wait time when asking questions.
- Avoid gender-biased language and stereotypical classroom jobs.
- If a boy wants to become a nurse and a girl has a passion for auto mechanics, encourage them to pursue their goals.
- Recognize that males and females can both learn to be courageous, caring, sensitive, humble, athletic, assertive, etc.

Curriculum and Instruction
- Use a variety of teaching methods to address different learning styles.
- Rather than grouping students by gender, encourage boys and girls to work together.
- Review curricula and instructional materials for gender bias.
- Avoid materials where females are invisible, shown as passive observers, or as a sideshow to the main event, e.g. a special chapter on "Women in Science."
- Use materials that show males and females from diverse backgrounds, including those in non-traditional gender roles.
- Make classes not just open to all students, but attractive to all.

Community Links
- Establish relationships with organizations that have developed successful out-of-school programs for girls in mathematics and science.
- Seek out opportunities in the private sector for student internships, including non-traditional jobs for both males and females.
- Consider bringing in community speakers of both genders, including those in non-traditional careers, to serve as role models.

References
1. www.titleix.info (and) www.nwlc.org/resource/battle-gender-equity-athletics-elementary-and-secondary-schools
2. www.aauw.org/files/2013/02/how-schools-shortchange-girls-executive-summary.pdf
3. http://ocrdata.ed.gov/Downloads/CRDC-School-Discipline-Snapshot.pdf (March 2014)
4. fortune.com/2019/05/16/fortune-500-female-ceos
5. Equity Online: www.edc.org > WEEA
6. National Women's History Project: www.nwhp.org
7. Education Next: http://educationnext.org/gender-gap
8. www.sadker.org/Still-Knocking.html (and) www.sadker.org/gendergames.html
9. Voyer and Voyer, Gender Differences in Scholastic Achievement: A Meta-Analysis, American Psychological Association, April 2014 (http://dx.doi.org/10.1037/a0036620)

8 Teacher Expectations & Student Achievement
A brief summary of the research. © Randie Gottlieb, Ed.D.

Research demonstrates that teachers interact differently with students who are expected to succeed, and that this can have a critical effect on achievement. Teachers of all backgrounds tend to have higher expectations for students who are white than they do for students of color. A student's gender, economic status and personality type can influence teacher expectations as well. Meanwhile, the number of low-income and students of color in our nation's schools continues to rise.

Ethnicity, Income and Achievement

National statistics show a wide gap in educational attainment between these students and their peers. They tend to have lower grades, higher failure and dropout rates, more frequent absences, a greater number of discipline referrals, and a lesser chance of entering or completing college. Some people claim that inherent racial differences are to blame for this achievement gap. However, the effects of poverty play a much larger role, and genetic research has demonstrated conclusively that there is only one human race. If test groups are matched for family socio-economic and educational background, there is no significant difference in scores.

Teacher Perceptions

1. Teachers tend to see students of color as lower achievers and white students as higher achievers—even when performance is identical.

2. White, physically attractive students from upper class backgrounds are consistently evaluated more favorably than students who are African American, unattractive, from a lower social class or with disabilities.

3. Teachers with low expectations tend to believe students are limited by their family background, home environment, etc. Teachers with high expectations tend to believe they can make a significant difference, regardless of a student's challenging background or environment.

Teachers Interact Differently

When a student isn't succeeding at school, a natural reaction is to look for a problem with the student. While this may be the case, there are undoubtedly other pieces to the puzzle, including the influence of the teacher. Trained classroom observers have identified a number of ways that teachers interact differently with low-expectation students. These observers aren't the only ones to notice the difference. Beginning as early as first grade, children are also aware of subtle non-verbal cues. When teachers have low expectations for certain students, they tend to:

- Demand less work from those students
- Call on them less often and ask easier questions
- Wait less time for them to answer
- Give them answers or call on others, rather than repeating questions or providing clues
- Give less approval
- Criticize those students more often for failure
- Reward inappropriate behavior

- Accept lower-quality or incorrect responses
- Give briefer, less informative feedback
- Give less freedom and responsibility in selecting their own work
- Not give the benefit of the doubt when grading assignments and tests
- Seat them farther away from the teacher
- Touch, nod and smile less

If students internalize these expectations, they expect less of themselves and put forth less effort.

What Can Be Done?

The first step is awareness of one's own attitudes and behaviors. It can be helpful for teachers to ask a colleague to observe and record their classroom interactions. This can involve a simple tally of the number of times the teacher performs a specific behavior and with whom.

Along with awareness, it is also important to understand the role of prejudice and stereotyping in forming expectations. While it is difficult to change beliefs and expectations just by thinking about them, it becomes easier if we begin by changing specific behaviors—one at a time. An instructional coach can identify which behaviors might be most effective, and suggest alternative strategies. Some examples are listed below.

Consider the Following Strategies

1. Develop a system for calling on students to ensure equitable attention for all. Don't just call on volunteers, which favors the more assertive students, often boys.
2. Encourage higher performance by asking higher-order questions—beyond rote memory.
3. Allow more time for students to answer questions (at least 5 seconds). Provide clues if they need help, or tell them the question for which their answer would be correct.
4. Use feedback to affirm or correct their performance. Some teachers feel it will embarrass students to correct them, but this also communicates that they don't think a student can learn.
5. Find something positive to praise in each student. When giving praise, specify the reasons why you feel they did well. This helps students understand exactly what the teacher liked about their work, and helps motivate them to repeat the effort.
6. When speaking with students, stand nearby and use appropriate touch and eye contact, responding in ways that show you are truly listening.
7. When disciplining students, check your own emotions. Remain calm and show courtesy and respect for the individual, even while correcting the negative behavior.
8. Give every student some individual attention and keep track of your efforts.
9. Show personal interest by spending time with challenging students outside the classroom at an activity of interest to them. Listen and observe, ask questions, try to understand how they view school and what motivates them. Find opportunities to show you care.
10. Seek advice from parents and other adults from the same cultural background as the student.
11. Intentionally communicate high expectations to all students and provide the necessary support.
12. Do not allow "in-class dropouts" who are mentally absent and who have conditioned teachers not to call on them. Let them know they are expected to participate and do well in school.

Conclusion: Expect More, Get More

Teacher expectations have a major effect on student achievement. Whether those expectations are high or low, they often become a self-fulfilling prophecy. A review of effective schools—including schools in high poverty areas with a majority of students of color, shows that they have one thing in common: high expectations for all. (References on p. 197) ∎

Some Current Approaches to MCE

© Randie Gottlieb, Ed.D.

1. Assimilation

Teaching diverse learners to assimilate into the mainstream culture

2. Cultural celebrations

Celebrating cultural foods and festivals, heroes and holidays

3. Human relations

Building community; teaching conflict resolution and communication skills

4. Ethnic studies

Learning about the history, current issues and contributions of specific cultures and ethnic groups

5. Culturally-responsive teaching

Using students' languages, cultures and experiences as a springboard for learning

6. Valuing diversity

Integrating multiple perspectives; learning about and from other groups; promoting unity in diversity

7. Self-examination

Examining our own biases and taking steps to become more inclusive and accepting of others

8. Academic support

Setting high expectations for all students and providing the support needed to achieve them

9. Social justice

Promoting human rights, anti-bias education and equity; learning about the issues and taking action

Notes: _____

_____

_____

_____

_____

_____

_____

_____

_____

_____

_____

_____

_____

_____

_____

_____

_____

_____

_____

_____

_____

_____

Creating Inclusive Classrooms and Schools

UnityWorks Training Institute

-1- **Five Shifts in Consciousness; AVID Program** Questions multicultural educators should be asking ourselves. The AVID Program.	**-2-** **10 Quick Ways to Analyze Children's Books for Bias** Guidelines for teachers and librarians on how to check for stereotypes, myths and distorted information.	**-3-** **A Model Kindergarten Class*** Culturally responsive teaching in a diverse classroom using images, stories and symbols.	**-4-** **Family Folklore: A Matter of the Heart** A middle school class learns about themselves and the world through their own family origins.
-5- **Fresh Takes: Video Project** Giving marginalized high school students a video camera and a voice for social action research.	**-6-** **A Teacher's Guide to Religion in the Public Schools** U.S. law and the study of religion, religious holidays, symbols, school prayer and after-school clubs.	**-7-** **Transgender Questions and Guidelines** Gender expression, safety, privacy, school climate, bathrooms, legal issues and FAQs.	**-8-** **Creating a Culture of Inclusion** Do all students feel welcome in school? Specific ways to create a welcoming climate for all.

* From Geneva Gay, *Culturally Sustaining Pedagogies: Teaching and Learning for Justice in a Changing World*, 2nd Edition, New York: Teachers College Press. © 2010 by Teachers College, Columbia University. All rights reserved. Reprinted by permission of the Publisher.

Five Shifts of Consciousness for Multicultural Educators

1

and the Questions We Should be Asking Ourselves

by Paul C. Gorski, gorski@edchange.org, www.edchange.org. Used with permission.

1. Advocating *equality* → Advocating *equity*

a. Does every student who walks into my school or classroom have an opportunity to achieve to her or his fullest capability regardless of race, ethnicity, sex, gender identity, sexual orientation, religion, socioeconomic status, home language, (dis)ability, and other social and cultural identifiers?

b. Do I understand that *equity* requires eliminating disparities in access to opportunities and resources—what some might call *fairness* or *justice*—and sometimes when we offer equality (giving everybody the same thing) we fail to meet this requirement?

c. When I advocate for equity in educational access do I take into account all types of "access"? Do I consider physical access as well as social, economic, and cultural access? For example, although all students in a particular high school might have "access" to upper-level mathematics classes in the sense that such classes are offered to anybody who has taken the prerequisites, do I consider in my equity advocacy the many ways in which some groups of students—women, for instance—are socialized not to pursue mathematics (or any other STEM field) as a course of study and that this, too, is about access?

2. Finding fault in disenfranchised families → Eradicating disenfranchising practices

a. Do I tend to find fault in students of color, low-income students, and other students and families from disenfranchised identity groups while failing to examine ways in which policies, practices and pedagogies, as well as larger societal factors (inequities in access to living wage work, health care, and safe and affordable housing, for instance) influence educational outcome disparities?

b. Do I tend to institute strategies for addressing these disparities which are aimed at "fixing" disenfranchised families rather than those conditions which disenfranchise families?

3. Color-blindness → Self-examination

a. Am I ignoring the existence of difference as a way to avoid addressing the difficult issues related to them?

b. Is color-blindness possible? And, if so, is it desirable when it denies people what may be important dimensions of their identities?

4. Learning about "other" cultures → Fighting for the rights of disenfranchised families

a. Although learning about my students' individual cultures is, indeed, a valuable pursuit, do I stop there or do I commit to and fight for their rights, such as the right not to be placed unjustly into low academic tracks (or to be tracked at all)?

b. "Other" than what?

5. Celebrating diversity → Committing to sustaining an equitable learning environment

a. Am I asking students who already are alienated by many aspects of education to celebrate a difference for which they may experience bias? If so, to whose benefit?

b. Might celebrating diversity in place of working toward a more equitable vision of multi-culturalism perpetuate the very inequities multicultural education is supposed to redress? ■

(1) The AVID Program

> AVID (Advancement Via Individual Determination) is a kindergarten through higher education program designed to close the achievement gap and to help students develop the skills they need to be successful in college. AVID's guiding principle is: Hold students accountable to the highest standards, provide academic and social support, and they will rise to the challenge. Today, AVID is regarded as one of the most effective educational reforms ever created by a classroom teacher. (www.avid.org)

Over 35 years ago, a judge's order forced suburban Clairemont High School in San Diego, Calif., to open its doors to 500 low-income students of color. At the time, the student body was over 95% white. In response, many of the wealthier families and several of the most experienced teachers left the school.

Clairemont decided to create special remedial classes for the new students, most of whom were at least two years behind grade level. Concerned about high dropout rates and low test scores, many schools would have done the same thing. However, Mary Catherine Swanson, chair of the high school's English department, disagreed.

She convinced the principal to enroll 30 of the incoming freshmen in the school's most difficult classes—if they agreed to meet with her for one period a day for tutoring and support. Four years later, to the surprise of everyone at Clairemont except herself, all 30 students went on to college.

Today, AVID impacts nearly 1.5 million students in 46 states and 16 countries, targeting middle-of-the-road students—those "B or C students who have shown potential," and many are the first in their family to go to college.[1]

Participation is voluntary and students demonstrate their commitment by choosing to enroll. They are then placed in their school's most advanced classes while meeting with their AVID tutor for one period each day. The tutor helps students develop critical thinking, literacy and math skills across all content areas. The program also places special emphasis on teamwork and study skills: what kinds of questions to ask in class, how to take notes, the best way to highlight a textbook, time management skills, and strategies for organizing their schoolwork. Middle and high school students can also explore different career paths, participate in field trips to local colleges, and learn about the college application process. To remain in the program, students must have satisfactory citizenship, good attendance, and a GPA of 2.0 or higher. ■

Summary by Randie Gottlieb. References below:

1. www.usnews.com/education/blogs/high-school-notes/2015/02/09/3-answers-for-high-school-parents-about-avid-classes
2. https://en.wikipedia.org/wiki/Advancement_Via_Individual_Determination
3. https://education.ucdavis.edu/boa-profile/mary-catherine-swanson

② Ten Quick Ways to Analyze Children's Books for Bias

Adapted by Randie Gottlieb from "Ten Quick Ways to Analyze Children's Books for Racism and Sexism" published by the Council on Interracial Books for Children, and from "Guide for Selecting Anti-Bias Children's Books" by Louise Derman-Sparks. Used with permission from Rethinking Schools, www.rethinkingschools.org.

Both in school and out, young children are exposed to racist and sexist attitudes. These attitudes—expressed repeatedly in books and other media—gradually distort their perceptions until stereotypes and myths about women, people of color, and other groups, are accepted as reality. While it is not necessary for every book in your collection to show diversity, every book should be accurate and respectful, and the collection itself should include a balance of diverse characters and themes. The following guidelines are offered as a starting point in evaluating children's books for bias.

1. Check the Illustrations

Look for Stereotypes. A stereotype is an over-simplified generalization about a particular group (e.g., gender, race, ethnicity, class, sexual orientation), which usually carries derogatory implications, e.g., "all Muslims are terrorists." Are the images stereotypical or accurate and respectful? Do they demean or ridicule characters because of their identity? Do all minority faces look alike, or are they depicted as individuals with distinctive features?

Look for Tokenism. Is there a symbolic effort to be inclusive by showing one member (or token) of a marginalized group, for example, only one black character among many white characters? Tokenism teaches children about who is or isn't important. It also shows them only one view of a group, rather than the diversity that exists among all groups. If there *are* people of color in the illustrations, do they look just like whites except for being colored in?

2. Check the Story Line

Who's Doing What? Are the whites in the story always the central figures? Do they possess the power, take the leadership roles, and make the important decisions—while others have secondary or subordinate parts? Are females, people of color, low-income families, or those with disabilities always depicted as needing help?

Standards for Success. Does it take "white" behavior standards for a person of color to get ahead? Is "making it" in the dominant white society projected as the ideal? To gain acceptance, do people from marginalized groups have to exhibit extraordinary qualities, or always be the ones to understand, forgive or change?

Resolution of Problems. How are problems presented and resolved in the story? Are marginalized groups considered to *be* the problem? Are the difficulties they face attributed to their own deficiencies or to an unjust system? Does the story settle for passive acceptance or does it encourage children to stand up for themselves and others when faced with injustice? If a problem is faced by a person of color, is it always resolved through the benevolent intervention of someone who is white?

Role of Females. Are males active doers and females passive observers? Are the achievements of girls and women based on their own initiative and intelligence, or are they due to their good looks, or to their relationship with males? Could the same story be told if the sex roles were reversed?

3. Look at the Lifestyles

Look for inaccuracies and inappropriateness in the depiction of other cultures. Are the lives of marginalized groups shown as "different" or in ways that contrast negatively with the unstated norm of white middle-class suburban life? Are people of color shown exclusively in ghettos, barrios or migrant camps? Does the setting reflect current realities, or assumptions from the past? Are the images and text oversimplified (e.g., quaint natives in costume), or do they offer genuine insights into the lifestyles of the characters in the story? Every group has diversity, including those who identify as white.

4. Note the Heroes

For many years, children's books showed only white male heroes and "safe" heroes from other groups—those who did not challenge the dominant culture of their time. Children also need to know about heroes from other groups—especially those who have worked or are currently working for social justice.

Does your book collection include a balance of people who have made important contributions to American life as well as to the world community? When heroes from other groups do appear, are they only admired because their efforts have benefited white people? The heroes we celebrate should reflect the diversity of our nation.

5. Who Is Invisible?

What children do *not* see in their storybooks and textbooks also sends a strong message about who matters and who doesn't in our society. Check your book collection for people who are commonly invisible: rural families, blue-collar workers, single or same-sex parents, homeless people, elders, indigenous families, Muslims and others.

6. Consider the Child's Self-Image

Does the book reinforce messages that teach children to feel superior or inferior because of their skin color, gender, family income, able-bodiedness or family structure? What effect can it have on African-American children to be continuously bombarded with images of the color white as the ultimate in cleanliness, beauty and virtue, while the color black is evil, dirty and menacing? What happens to a girl's self-image if she is not fair-skinned and slim?

Will all the children you serve see themselves and their family positively reflected in your book collection? Are there one or more role models with whom they can identify—including those with mixed heritage, who have disabilities, who are adopted, bilingual or living in poverty? Does your collection include the diversity beyond your classroom walls?

7. Consider the Author and Illustrator

In the past, most children's book authors and illustrators were white and middle class. As a result, a single ethnocentric perspective has dominated children's literature. We now have many titles by and about those from other backgrounds. If a book is not about people or events from the author's or illustrator's background, what specifically qualifies them as the creators of that book? What is their attitude toward the story's characters?

8. Watch for Loaded Words

A word is loaded when it demeans people or makes them invisible because of their identity. Examples of loaded adjectives that can carry racist messages when applied to people of color include: *savage, primitive, lazy, superstitious, treacherous, crafty, inscrutable* and *backward*.

Also look for sexist language that excludes or demeans women, for example, the generic use of *man* to stand for females as well. The following examples show how sexist language can usually be avoided: *ancestors* instead of *forefathers*, *firefighters* instead of *firemen*, *the human family* instead of *the family of man*.

9. Look at the Copyright Date

Books on "minority" themes suddenly began appearing in the mid-1960s to meet a new market demand. Most of these books were still written by white authors, edited by white editors, published by white publishers, and reflected a "white point of view." Although a recent copyright date is no guarantee of a book's relevance or sensitivity, more recent publications tend to better reflect the realities of a multicultural society, and the number of accurate and respectful books incorporating diversity has increased significantly.

10. What About the Classics?

Folk and fairy tales have long been a mainstay of children's literature, but many carry messages that are sexist or racist. Sleeping Beauty must be rescued by the handsome prince. The Ugly Duckling is taught: "Stick to your own kind." Rather than advocating for the removal of such stories, or using them despite their biased messages, we can use them as tools for helping children to recognize stereotyping and to think critically, as an important element in teaching about social justice. ∎

The kindergarten class Lois teaches is comprised of immigrant and first-generation U.S. students from many countries, as well as a mixture of different native ethnic groups. Consequently, there is a lot of ethnic, racial, cultural and linguistic diversity present. Looking into her classroom provides a glimpse of how culturally responsive teaching can be accomplished through the use of visual imagery and symbols. ...As we take a quick tour of this classroom, we witness the following:

Attached to the entrance door is a huge welcome sign brightly decorated with the children's own art. The sign reads "Welcome to Our Academic Home." This message is accompanied by a group photograph of the members of the class and "welcome" in different languages (Spanish, Japanese, German, French, various U.S. dialects, etc.). Stepping inside the room, one is bombarded with an incredibly rich and wide range of ethnically and culturally diverse images. Maps of the world and the United States are prominently displayed on the front wall, under the heading "We Come from Many Places." Strings connect different parts of the world to the United States. They represent the countries of origin of the families and/or ethnic groups of the students in the class. A display in another corner of the room is labeled "Our Many Different Faces." It includes a montage of close-up facial photographs of the members of the class. These are surrounded by pictures of adults from different ethnic groups in ceremonial dress for various rites of passage (e.g., marriage, adulthood, baptism) and occupations (clergy, doctors, construction workers, dancers).

The room's "Reading Center" is a prototype of multicultural children's literature—a culturally responsive librarian's dream!...Books, poems, comics, song lyrics, posters, magazines, and newspapers beckon the students to discover and read about the histories, families, myths, folktales, travels, troubles, triumphs, experiences, and daily lives of a wide variety of Asian, African, European, Middle Eastern, Latino, Native American, and Pacific Islander groups and individuals. Audio- and videotapes are liberally sprinkled among these items, including

music, books on tape, storytelling, and television programs. Others look like student productions. In the midst of all these media materials, a video camera and [an audio] recorder stand in readiness for use. Another curious item captures the attention. It is a pile of tattered, well-used photo albums. These resources invite students to explore the past, to reflect on the present, to imagine the future.

The extent and quality of this collection of materials prompt the question, "Lois, how did you come by all of this?" She credits parents for the accomplishment. At the beginning of the academic year, she gets [them] to make a contractual agreement to donate two books or other forms of media to the class collection. One of these books is to be about their own ethnic group and the other about some other group that they either use with their children at home or would like their children to learn about in school. The families are given credit for their contributions by having each item stamped "Donated by_____." When the collection becomes too large to be easily accommodated in the classroom, or the students "outgrow it," some of the items are donated to the school library or community agencies. This is a class project, with the students deciding which items they will keep and which they will give away....The recipients must agree to acknowledge the donors with the credit line "Donated by the Kindergarten Class of Room____ at Elementary School."

Lois is a strong believer in "representative ethnic imagery." She is very conscientious about ensuring that the visual depictions of ethnic groups and individuals in her classroom are accurate, authentic, and pluralistic. She explains that she wants students to readily recognize who the ethnic visuals represent rather than having to wonder....She also wants the students to be exposed to a wide variety of images within and among groups to avoid ethnic stereotyping. To assist the students with this, all of the pictures...include personal and ethnic identities. These read, "My name is _____; I am _____" [ethnic group]. Lois justifies this protocol by simply saying, "Students need to know that it's OK to recognize other people's ethnicity and to expect others to acknowledge theirs. Ethnicity is an important feature of our personal identities."

Two other permanent…displays exist in this stimulating, intellectually invigorating, and culturally diverse classroom. One is entitled "We Can Do Many Things." Here are images, samples, and symbols of the contributions and accomplishments of different ethnic groups, such as crafts, arts, science, technology, medicine, and music. They include children and adults of different ages, famous and common folks, profound achievements, and regular, daily occurrences.

For example, there is one photograph of three students who have been especially helpful to classmates from other ethnic groups and another of six great-grandparents who are 75 years of age or older. The master [soundtrack] representing different ethnic groups' contributions to music includes excerpts from operas, jazz, rap, spirituals, movie sound tracks, country, pop, and children's songs. The names of other individuals are accompanied by miniature samples of their contributions. There is the athlete with a little basketball, but it's refreshing to see that she is a member of the 1996 U.S. Olympic team, and Venus and Serena are there with their little tennis rackets. Some kernels of corn appear next to Native Americans, and a little make-believe heart operation kit is connected to African Americans.

The other permanent display is a multicultural alphabet streamer. Different ethnic groups and contributions are associated with each of the letters…For example, "Jamaican" and "Japanese American," as well as "jazz" appear under the letter J, and "lasso" and "Latino" appear under L.

The tour of this classroom also offers a glimpse into how Lois incorporates the ethnically diverse symbols into her formal instruction. Small groups of students are working on different skills. As Lois circulates among them, activities in the reading and math groups are riveting. It is Carlos's turn to select the book to be read for story time. He chooses one about a Japanese American family. Lois asks him to tell the group why he made this choice. Carlos explains that he had seen Yukiko (a classmate) at McDonald's over the weekend, and he wanted to do something nice for her by reading "her" book.

…Before Lois begins to read the story, she tells the students a little about this ethnic group, like the proper name, its country of origin, some symbol of its culture…and where large numbers of its members live in the United States. She asks if anyone can find Japan and California on the maps. She helps the group locate these places.

As the students return to their places and settle down for the story, we hear Lois asking, "If we wanted to go to the places where there are a lot of Japanese Americans, how would we get there? Who would like to go?" Several hands pop up quickly at the thought of such an imagined journey….Once this "context setting" is completed, Lois proceeds through a reading of the book. She pauses frequently to probe the students' understanding…, to examine their feelings, and to predict upcoming developments in the story.

In math, the students are practicing bilingual counting… On this occasion, they are learning to count to 10 in Spanish… One student points to the words as the others say them aloud. After some giggling and gentle consternation about their pronunciation, Lois compliments the students' efforts… Tamika reminds everyone that Rosita speaks Spanish at home and announces, with conviction, "I bet she can say those words real good." Lois asks Rosita if she would like to give it a try. After a little encouragement from other members of the group, she agrees. Lois tells the group that Rosita is now the teacher and the other students are to practice saying the words as she does.

Symbols are powerful conveyers of meaning, as Lois's classroom attests. Her students are inundated with positive images and interactions with ethnic and cultural diversity. They learn about and celebrate their own and one another's identities and abilities, while simultaneously being invited to extend the boundaries of their knowledge and skills. All of this occurs in a warm, supportive, affirming, and illuminating classroom climate…This type of instruction is very conducive to high levels of many different kinds of achievement for students from all ethnic groups. ■

Family Folklore
A Matter of the Heart

Mary Mercer Krogness, Language Arts Journal, Vol. 64, No. 8, p.808-818.
Used with permission from the National Council of Teachers of English.

> *Dear parents: Our class is learning about the world by finding
> out about countries and cultures represented in our student body.
> Please help us to get started by filling out this family tree....*

Folk, all of us—kids, parents, siblings, grandparents, aunts, uncles, cousins, extended families, even teachers—can be a natural community...My students and I began the study of family folklore by talking about ourselves, where we'd come from, the need for each of us to find his or her beginnings—"roots" from Alex Haley's point of view; letting our family origins become the stimuli for talking, reading and writing. What did we bring with us? What were the cultural and linguistic traditions that each of us carried to class each day?

Ours is considered to be a homogeneous class. We are, from all outward appearances, uniformly well-groomed and self-possessed. But during the course of the family folklore project, as we uncovered fragments of our past, I became aware of our cultural differences, sometimes subtle but nonetheless profound.

The richness of this project, we discovered, was derived from family study and thus self-discovery, but also from the pain of acknowledging that we were not only different, we were unequal; that each of us had come into a different world...

The study included collecting real stories (i.e., emigration stories), tall tales, jokes, super-stitions, remedies, recipes and the like from our families.... A new sense of community began to develop within our classroom and beyond its walls as the children, their parents, and I uncovered new bits and pieces of information that we'd been told or found while listening to family tales and videos or looking through old family photo albums, documents and diaries.

[One mother wrote] "I became so interested in this project that I made up family history folders for each of my children to keep and pass on."

[From a student] "Some of the information I gathered from my grandparents would have been lost forever if I hadn't collected it."

[From another parent] "Getting a sense of the strength, courage and intelligence that the children carry in their genes—not only from kings, pilgrims and statesmen—but from the more recent immigrants, is important. This study gives children a feeling of confidence, a feeling of generations and belonging."

...None of us could have imagined late in November what, through deep personal investment, we knew in March about our classmates and ourselves. I could only have anticipated that for some of us wounds would be opened as we became committed to uncovering our families' past.

…My children's backgrounds were the primary stimuli for the stories, songs, poems, plays, scrapbooks, diaries, tabloids, newspapers, cartoons and a class cookbook that we created and had printed professionally. The voices are authentic; interest among students and their families certainly was more intense than I would have imagined.

There's no prescribed scope and sequence or teacher's manual to lean on. We began by developing a set of questions that served as a basis for interviewing family members. Here are a few:

- Where did the family come from? When? Why?
- Where in America did they settle? Why?
- What kinds of work did they do?
- What were some of the difficulties that they experienced?
- What were some of their disappointments and dreams?

Several storytellers came to our classroom. The school librarian provided plenty of films and books…The art of language was flourishing for now we brought a richer understanding of characters to literature that we read…Finally we staged a folk fair for our families and 225 schoolmates and their teachers to display our wares.

The effects of cultural diversity on language and learning are more powerful than perhaps are apparent…Considering seriously the rich diversity of our students and their languages, and thereby valuing their traditions, gives impetus to designing curricula—curricula that by design make talking and writing together a way of life, tools for living and learning together, and touchstones for our humanness. ■

– A Note from UnityWorks –

The family is the primary unit of society where culture is passed down and socialization takes place. Family folklore is concerned with traditional culture transmitted within a family group. Folklore can include material items such as family photos, diplomas, letters, journals, recipes, handicrafts and objects that serve as reminders of significant family events. It can also include family stories, songs, expressions and holiday customs that help define the values and a common identity for the family unit.

Today, many students come from a traditional family consisting of a mother, father and children. For others, the definition of family includes single parents, grandparents, same-sex couples, adopted children, blended families and more. Some students may not live in a stable family group, so alternatives should be given when making this assignment. Such students, for example, might interview someone from a family they admire, and report on that family's folklore.

Fresh Takes

Reprinted with permission of Teaching Tolerance,
a project of the Southern Poverty Law Center, www.tolerance.org

"We're not here tonight to listen to the adults," Orlando tells the audience. "We really want to hear what young people have to say." He holds up a videotape, a short documentary he and his colleagues—Alexis, Kellon and Christine—are producing about the criminal justice system. They are here tonight in a makeshift screening room in midtown Manhattan representing Youth Organizer Television (Yo!-TV), and are eager to exhibit their work before an audience of their peers—approximately 25 young…media artists.

by Tim Walker

As a group, this small community embodies not only the…racial and cultural diversity of New York City, but also the determination of many disadvantaged teenagers to bring their ideas and opinions to the public forum. For these young people, ages 12 to 20, the documentaries…they create with video technology function as high-tech calls to arms to promote dialogue, peer learning and social activism….While the videos varied in subject, tone and technical sophistication, each relayed a distinct, hard-hitting message.

"We call ours *Tough on Crime, Tough on Our Kind*," announces Orlando. "In it we examine how the criminal justice system targets young people of color." "Like all of you, we see a lot of what is wrong in our neighborhoods," he continues. "But so far the solutions have also been wrong…" Orlando then hands the tape to Kellon, who pushes it into the VCR and hits Play.

Tough on Crime opens with an interrogation. A young Latino male, framed in a tight close-up, peers directly into the camera and challenges the viewer: "Why are young people of color being sent to prison when others are not being treated the same?"… "Why doesn't the system do anything to fix the problems that create crime?"

Tough on Crime then goes on to examine how three young people…became entangled in the juvenile justice system. The teenagers tell their own stories, candidly describing how their life circumstances compelled them to make poor choices. These narratives are interspersed with perspectives of city officials, social workers and community activists…

Tough on Crime covers a lot of ground in its 15 minutes, but its message comes through undiminished. And it's obvious, judging by the hands raised quickly in unison after the tape is ejected from the VCR, that the video has struck a chord with the audience. One young girl comments on how the people and situations portrayed in the documentary could have easily taken place in any city or town in the U.S. This video should be taken on the road, says another, and suggests schools and community organizations that would welcome it. Other onlookers offer suggestions and criticisms about the video's technical choices and pacing. All in all, the Yo!-TV team seems pleased that the audience has validated their hard work.

"That's part of the appeal of video education and peer filmmaking," explains Susan Siegel, co-founder of the Global Action Project (G.A.P.), a local media arts organization that is hosting tonight's screening. "Kids thrive off each other's feedback. They have respect for each other's work. They know the kind of commitment it takes to produce a short video. It's also refreshing for them to learn from someone closer in age."

For Siegel and other educators, the empowering effect and the impact on self-esteem of peer filmmaking can't be overstated, especially when scapegoating and stereotyping of young people by the news and entertainment industry have reached new intensity. Self-representation of young people in the media can neutralize negative images. But the merits don't end there.

Many experts have praised youth-produced videos as highly effective tools to help teenagers find their voices and use them to create change in their communities. Whether in a city of 8 million or a rural community in the Midwest, neighborhoods are often underused laboratories for learning. Marginalized youth, equipped with a video camera, can transform issues that once hobbled their academic and social development—racism, crime, stereotypes, poverty—into opportunities for research, problem-solving and social action.

Images and Sounds of Activism: ...G.A.P.'s Urban Voices is an after-school program that trains low-income youth to research, write and produce videos on issues that are important to them and their communities. The students learn how to develop and facilitate workshops, using their videos to educate their peers on important social issues... The filmmakers must develop the trust in themselves and others who may share different points of view. It's wondrous to watch students become teachers.

"...Adults are the decision makers," [Kellon says], "the people in power. We need to tell them what is going on in our community....With a camera, you can look at something with a fresh perspective and see familiar things in a new way. The kids in the neighborhood who saw my video seemed galvanized. That's what video can do: It presents a picture, an issue to address, and then asks, 'OK, so what are you going to do about it?'" ...Once complete, the videotape becomes a tool for social action....*Tough on Crime* will be shown at a human rights film festival in a couple of weeks and at community organizations after that.

Whoever Controls the Tape Controls the Message: Many experts are urging educators to embrace both the "deconstruction" and construction of media. Dissecting and analyzing a commercial, news report or movie is an indispensable activity, but left unaccompanied, could frame the media exclusively as something to be distrusted. Empowering students, on the other hand, to produce their own positive messages not only enriches their understanding of various media but also introduces them to powerful communication tools...

"Media literacy is still a young discipline struggling to find its place," says Steve Goodman. "One of the first steps for schools is to acknowledge that print isn't the only form of literacy—media is the language of our popular culture. While there's a definite growth in interest, schools need to make the right choices when they decide to invest in production." Many programs, for example, tend to stress the technological/vocational aspects of the trade, not the content....While such an approach may provide valuable vocational skills and fun for the students...it's gravely lacking as a form of expression, community engagement and social activism...

Obstacles emerge over what is and is not appropriate content for students to explore. Similar to the dilemmas they face with school newspapers, educators sometimes cringe at the thought of placing video cameras in the hands of their students.

"When you give teenagers the opportunity to use their own voices, [explains Hobbs], they very well might say something that makes adults uncomfortable. They might point out the hypocrisies or fallacies of the adult-dominated society, or they might...make videos that are misogynistic, racist and violent." Guidance from instructors who know how to foster student creativity and channel it constructively, therefore, becomes absolutely crucial...

Orlando removes the videotape from his knapsack and taps it with his index finger. "This is our reality." ■

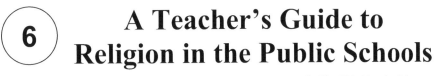

A Teacher's Guide to Religion in the Public Schools

Charles C. Haynes, the First Amendment Center, Nashville, TN. Used with permission.

A statement endorsed by the National Education Association, American Federation of Teachers, National School Boards Association, Association for Supervision and Curriculum Development, National PTA, American Association of School Administrators, American Jewish Congress, Anti-Defamation League, Catholic League for Religious and Civil Rights, Christian Educators Association, Council on Islamic Education, and more.

"Congress shall make no law respecting an establishment of religion, or prohibiting the free exercise thereof…"

—First Amendment to the U.S. Constitution

Public schools may not inculcate nor inhibit religion. They must be places where religion and religious conviction are treated with fairness and respect. Public schools uphold the First Amendment when they protect the religious liberty rights of students of all faiths or none. Schools demonstrate fairness when they ensure that the curriculum includes study about religion, where appropriate, as an important part of a complete education.

Is it constitutional to teach about religion? Yes. In the 1960s school prayer cases (that prompted rulings against state-sponsored school prayer and Bible reading), the U.S. Supreme Court indicated that public school education may include teaching about religion. In *Abington v. Schempp*, Associate Justice Tom Clark wrote for the Court:

> It might well be said that one's education is not complete without a study of comparative religion or the history of religion and its relationship to the advancement of civilization…

Why should study about religion be included in the curriculum? Because religion plays a significant role in history and society, study about religion is essential to understanding both the nation and the world…Study about religion is also important if students are to value religious liberty, the first freedom guaranteed in the Bill of Rights. Moreover, knowledge of the roles of religion in the past and present promotes cross-cultural understanding essential to democracy and world peace.

How should I teach about religion? The answer to the "how" question begins with a clear understanding of the crucial difference between the teaching of religion…and teaching about religion. The school's approach to religion [should be] *academic*, not *devotional*. The school may *expose* students to a diversity of religious views, but may not *impose* any particular view.

But public-school teachers are required by the First Amendment to teach about religion fairly and objectively, neither promoting nor denigrating religion in general or specific religious groups in particular. When discussing religion, many teachers guard against injecting personal religious beliefs by teaching through attribution (e.g., by using such phrases as "most Buddhists believe…" or "according to the Hebrew scriptures…").

How should I treat religious holidays in the classroom? Teachers must be alert to the distinction between teaching about religious holidays, which is permissible, and celebrating religious holidays, which is not…Information about holidays may focus on how and when they are celebrated, their origins, histories and generally agreed-upon meanings.

The use of religious symbols …The use of religious symbols, provided they are used only as examples of cultural or religious heritage, is permissible as a teaching aid or resource. Religious symbols may be displayed only on a temporary basis as part of the academic lesson being studied. Students may choose to create artwork with religious symbols, but teachers should not assign or suggest such creations.

…sacred music may be sung or played as part of the academic study of music…Concerts should avoid programs dominated by religious music, especially when these coincide with a particular religious holiday.

What is the relationship between religion and character education? …Teachers must remain neutral concerning religion, neutral among religions, and neutral between religion and non-religion. But this does not mean that teachers should be neutral concerning civic virtue or moral character. Teachers should teach the personal and civic virtues widely held in our society, such as honesty, caring, fairness and integrity. They must do so without either invoking religious authority or denigrating the religious or philosophical commitments of students and parents.

May I pray or otherwise practice my faith while at school? As employees of the government, public-school teachers are subject to the Establishment Clause of the First Amendment and thus required to be neutral concerning religion while carrying out their duties as teachers. That means, for example, that teachers do not have the right to pray with or in the presence of students during the school day…Outside of their school responsibilities, public-school teachers are free like other citizens to teach or otherwise participate in their local religious community.

Teachers are permitted to wear non-obtrusive jewelry, such as a cross or Star of David. But teachers should not wear clothing with a proselytizing message (e.g., a "Jesus Saves" T-shirt).

How do I respond if students ask about my religious beliefs? Some teachers prefer not to answer the question, stating that it is inappropriate for a teacher to inject personal beliefs into the discussion. Other teachers may choose to answer the question straightforwardly and succinctly in the interest of an open and honest classroom environment… In any case, the teacher may answer at most with a brief statement of personal belief—but may not turn the question into an opportunity to proselytize for or against religion.

May students express religious views in public schools? Students have the right to pray individually or in groups or to discuss their religious views with their peers so long as they are not disruptive…However, the right to engage in voluntary prayer does not include, for example, the right to have a captive audience listen or to compel other students to participate.

May students form extracurricular religious clubs? The Equal Access Act passed by Congress in 1984 ensures that students in secondary public schools may form religious clubs, including Bible clubs, if the school allows other "non-curriculum-related groups."…According to the Act, outsiders may not "direct, conduct, control, or regularly attend" student religious clubs, and teachers acting as monitors may be present at religious meetings in a non-participatory capacity only. ■

7 Transgender Questions & Guidelines

© Randie Gottlieb, Ed.D.

Transgender: A person who identifies differently than their sex at birth.

Recent concerns about transgender students using bathrooms consistent with their gender identity, rather than their sex at birth, have raised many questions for students, educators and parents. Common areas of concern include safety, privacy, school climate and legal issues. Celebrities like Caitlyn Jenner have helped to raise awareness, but transgender individuals (particularly transgender women of color) are among the most at-risk segments of our society.[1]

In an annual survey of more than 7,000 middle and high school students, the Gay, Lesbian & Straight Education Network (GLSEN) found that schools nationwide are hostile environments for many LGBT students, including "74% who were verbally harassed in the past year because of their sexual orientation and 55% because of their gender expression. As a result of feeling unsafe or uncomfortable, 30% missed at least one day of school in the past month."[2]

Federal Guidelines

In May 2016, the U.S. Departments of Education and Justice called on the nearly 100,000 public schools nationwide to allow transgender students to use the bathroom that matches their gender identity, as a condition for receiving federal funds.

While schools would be permitted to offer single-use restrooms to students seeking additional privacy (e.g., for cultural or religious reasons or a particular health issue), they could not *require* transgender students to use such facilities if their classmates were not required to do so as well. A school could, however, make individual-user options available to all students who voluntarily seek additional privacy. The letter notes that "a school's Title IX obligation to ensure nondiscrimination on the basis of sex requires schools to provide transgender students equal access to educational programs and activities even in circumstances in which other students, parents or community members raise objections or concerns. As is consistently recognized in civil rights cases, the desire to accommodate others' discomfort cannot justify a policy that singles out and disadvantages a particular class of students."[3]

Shortly after this policy was adopted, 13 states filed suit, accusing the government of a "massive social experiment" that threatens the safety of children.[4] The policy was rescinded in Feb. 2017.

Battle of the Bathrooms

In practice, however, a transgender person is much more likely to be the victim of violence. Many such students avoid using public bathrooms out of fear that another student will hurt them. The consequences can be severe, impacting children's physical and emotional health and their ability to learn.[5]

It is understandable for people to feel uncomfortable with something new. Educators charged with addressing these concerns would do well to engage their communities in a civil, well-informed conversation, reinforcing the idea that our first priority is making sure every child is safe at school.

Personal stories can help to dispel stereotypes and prejudice, and to increase understanding and empathy. See the "eclectablog" website (reference #1 below) for a series of real life stories from transgender people and their families.

Common Questions Answered

A new document from Gender Spectrum, "Transgender Students and School Bathrooms: Frequently Asked Questions,"[5] addresses common questions that arise for school and district leaders as they work to create gender-inclusive school environments and respond to concerns raised by the community. Included are thoughtful responses to questions such as:

- Why can't transgender students just use a private bathroom?
- What if a student pretends to be transgender in order to enter another bathroom?
- What if my child doesn't feel safe or comfortable in a bathroom with a transgender student?
- Are there specific legal requirements that schools and districts need to know?
- How can I respond to parents who are genuinely concerned?

Anticipating these concerns and providing concrete responses will allow educators to respond successfully to most situations related to the topic. This resource is endorsed by the American School Counselor Association, both National Associations of School Principals (elementary and secondary), and the National Association of School Psychologists.

In addition, the National Association of Secondary School Principals (NASSP) has produced an excellent position paper on transgender students.[6] It includes detailed recommendations for district policy makers and school leaders.

One Person's Experience

After she came out as a transwoman, Meredith Russo's co-workers took it in stride, but her boss told her she had to use the men's room. "Every time I encountered men in the bathroom in my skirt and makeup," she said, "they'd act startled, assuming they'd accidentally entered the women's room, and then glare at me or angrily insist I should be in the women's room." It got so bad that she stopped going to the bathroom at work altogether.

While some people raise the fear of male predators in dresses, there is no evidence that this is a statistically significant concern. However, putting "people who now have a woman's identity and appearance in men's rooms, and transmen with beards and muscles in women's rooms, [makes] everyone unhappy, and people like me afraid we'll be assaulted, fired, or arrested. Please: We are much more frightened of you than you are of us." (Ref: The Week, 3 June 2016) ■

References
1. www.eclectablog.com/2016/03/introducing-a-story-series-about-the-lives-of-transgender-people.html
2. www.glsen.org/article/glsen-releases-new-national-school-climate-survey
3. www2.ed.gov/about/offices/list/ocr/letters/colleague-201605-title-ix-transgender.pdf
4. www.nytimes.com/2016/05/26/us/states-texas-sue-obama-administration-over-transgender-bathroom-policy.html?_r=0
5. www.genderspectrum.org/bathroomfaq
6. www.nassp.org/who-we-are/board-of-directors/position-statements/transgender-students?SSO=true
7. Small Towns Making a Big Stand: http://embrace.today
8. transequality.org/school-action-center
9. www.nytimes.com/2017/02/24/us/transgender-bathroom-law.html

⑧ Creating a Culture of Inclusion

© Randie Gottlieb, Ed.D.

All classrooms are diverse in many ways. In addition to immigrant students who may bring different languages and cultures to campus, students also bring differences in religion, gender, skin color, sexual orientation, family situation, economic status, social class and dietary restrictions. Some students are athletic; some are not. Some are attractive; some less so. Some read well; others poorly. Some have abusive parents, or are affected by alcohol, drugs, divorce, homelessness, or a serious medical condition. Some students have jobs, some have disabilities, some help raise younger siblings, some are thin or overweight, outgoing or shy.

Do all of these students fit in? Are English language learners tested quickly and placed in appropriate programs with the necessary support? Or is academic potential judged by poor clothing, limited English or immigrant status? Do other students accept those who are different, or are they labeled, teased, bullied and excluded? Children and teens can be cruel to those who do not fit in with the popular crowd.

How can we create a welcoming climate for all? We can teach all students to feel comfortable with people from diverse backgrounds; to act with courage to stop negative behavior; to actively include those who are different; and to treat others with kindness and respect. And we can create a more inclusive culture in our school.

Inclusion does not mean dumping all students into the regular classroom with no teacher preparation or support. Inclusion means more than tolerance, or even acceptance. It means being appreciated as a valued part of a shared community. It means knowing that we're all connected, that we all belong. The goal of an inclusive classroom is not to ignore or eliminate differences, but to acknowledge and use them to create a cooperative community that works for all.

We don't need to sacrifice reading and math to teach cooperation and inclusion. We can structure reading and math as cooperative activities in themselves. We can teach cooperative skills, such as listening, sharing, peer teaching, group decision-making, conflict resolution, and the art of encouragement. Students can study examples of cooperation in history, science and other subjects. We can employ more inclusive models of curriculum, instruction and assessment. We can restructure ways that students are grouped and rewarded. We can honor the language and cultural experiences that students bring to the classroom, and use these as springboards for academic learning.

Time spent building community is not wasted. It lays the foundation for academic success. If students feel safe and accepted, they will be free to learn. This allows teachers to spend more time teaching and less time dealing with conflict and trauma. Teaching cooperation and inclusion should not be add-ons. There are many teachable moments every day.

A Few Examples of Inclusion

Adapted from *Because We Can Change The World,* Mara Sapon-Shevin, p. 62, 64, 84, 93. Used with permission.

(1) Marta, a third-grader, is excited about the upcoming puppet show her class is doing. Some children have written the script, others have designed the scenery, a few will work the puppets, and some will make programs and sell tickets. Marta, **who uses a wheelchair** and a computerized touch talker, is the play's narrator. When it is her turn to talk, Marta activates the touch talker and the next piece of the story plays.

(2) In Mr. Watkin's class, Valentine's Day is celebrated as a day of friendship. Last year, there was fierce competition about who got the most valentines and many children had hurt feelings, so Mr. Watkins now has another system. Each student cluster (four to five students who sit together) is assigned to plan a "surprise treat" for another cluster, and is required to use resources available in the room or with no cost.

(3) Linda has diabetes. In classroom A, the teacher buys some sugar-free cookies for the class party, and quietly hands those to Linda so the other students will not see. In classroom B, all the students *know* that Linda has diabetes, and they understand when and why she takes insulin. When planning the class party, the students make a list of snacks that everyone can eat. They include Linda's needs as well as those of Sarah who is a vegetarian, Nicolas who is allergic to wheat, and Amman who does not eat pork. The goal is not to hide Linda's unique needs, but to think about her as both an individual and a member of a cohesive, classroom community.

(4) A seventh-grade class completed an Accessibility Checklist for their school. They discovered it was impossible for students in wheelchairs to take classes above the first floor. They wrote letters to the principal and the school board, detailing what they found, why it mattered, and what should be done about it. As a follow-up activity, they visited theaters, restaurants and stores in the community, and wrote letters to those that were inaccessible. Rather than writing pretend letters to nonexistent businesses (as suggested by the school's standard curriculum), students learned real advocacy skills, and discovered their own power to change things that are unfair.

(5) Another class generated its own Yellow Pages, with listings of the things students could teach or share. The teacher helped students generate ideas, and students wrote their own classified ads for skills, interests and needs. This was particularly effective for students who felt they were not good at anything. Help Offered ads might look like this:

> Do you have trouble getting organized at school? I can help. I have a system for recording homework and I'll share it with you. I also know some good memory tricks. See Carlos.

> Want to learn origami? I can show you how to fold swans, frogs & bears. After you've learned the basics, I can teach you more complicated animals with moving parts. See Hiriko.

(6) One school posted a "Help" board in the teachers' lounge, and soon had ads like these:

> I need suggestions for reading & writing activities for two students from Vietnam with limited English. If you have any materials or ideas, I'd really appreciate your help. See Karen Boyd, Rm. 24.

> Want to get parents more involved in the classroom? I've come up with some successful strategies, especially for those hard-to-reach parents. See Elena Sanchez, Rm. 33.

Paper PowerPoint - Due Day 5

Your team has five minutes to prepare a "Paper PowerPoint" on one of the sections below. Use the markers and blank paper to create up to five "slides" using text and/or images to answer the questions. Tomorrow, your team will have 1-2 minutes to present your slides during the morning review.

Item	Day 4 Review Topics
A	• Define "achievement gap" and give some reasons for it. • What is the relationship between income and education?
B	• How do teacher expectations affect student achievement? • How do teachers interact differently with high- and low-expectation students?
C	• What are some institutional barriers to equity and achievement? • Briefly define each one.
D	• What is the school-to-prison pipeline? • Why is it called "the new Jim Crow," and what can educators do about it?
E	• How would you respond to the following statement? *"Black and Hispanic students do worse in school due to a lack of motivation, limited parental involvement, and poor cultural values."*
F	• What is the difference between equality and equity? Give an example. • Give examples of specific programs and strategies that can increase equity and student achievement.

For 5 teams, combine topics A & E.
For 7 teams, add G: **What is the "culture of poverty" and what can educators do about it?**
For 8 teams, add G and H: **What is the ELL gap, and how can we increase success for our ELL students?**

Notes:

_____

_____

_____

_____

_____

_____

_____

_____

_____

_____

_____

_____

_____

_____

_____

_____

_____

_____

_____

PART V

Diversity Challenges & Solutions

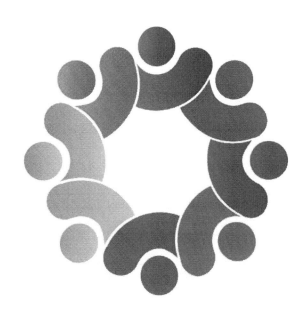

DIVERSITY BASICS
- Key concepts and vocabulary
- Dimensions of diversity
- Social justice, civil and human rights
- Elements of culture and communication style
- The value of diversity and the need for unity
- From ethnocentrism and assimilation to unity in diversity

THE REALITY OF RACE
- What is race and how many races are there?
- How do we get our skin color?
- Genetics, eugenics and the family tree
- Our stories

PREJUDICE, POWER AND PRIVILEGE
- Prejudice: causes, consequences and cures
- Racism, discrimination and stereotypes in society today
- Disproportionate discipline and the school-to-prison pipeline
- Microaggressions and colorblindness
- Missing chapters, counter-narratives
- U.S. historical perspectives, laws and policies
- Tribal history and culture
- Unconscious bias, intent vs. impact
- The power of language

EQUITY, EXPECTATIONS AND ACHIEVEMENT
- Achievement gap, opportunity gap, potential gap, diversity gap
- School experiences of mainstream and marginalized students
- Teacher expectations and student achievement
- Institutional barriers to equity and achievement
- Poverty, gender, religion, LGBT and ELL topics
- Equality vs. equity

MODELS OF UNITY AND ACTION
- Authentic voices, multiple perspectives, involving parents and community
- Stages of organizational development, diversity challenges and solutions
- Culturally-responsive pedagogy: curriculum, instruction, assessment
- Creating a culture of inclusion: successful models and strategies
- Multicultural assessment of our organization
- Creating a diversity action plan

Notes: _____

_____

_____

_____

_____

_____

_____

_____

_____

_____

_____

_____

_____

_____

_____

_____

_____

_____

_____

_____

_____

_____

1. What is the difference between ethnocentrism, assimilation and unity in diversity?

2. What is culturally responsive teaching, and how can it improve school climate and student learning?

3. Briefly define these terms and give an example of each:
   a. diversity
   b. multiple perspectives
   c. mirrors and windows
   d. missing chapters
   e. counter-narratives
   f. equality
   g. equity

4. Define culture and explain the difference between deep and surface culture. How might cultural differences affect interactions and experiences in school?

5. Briefly define these terms and give an example of each:
   a. prejudice
   b. discrimination
   c. microaggressions
   d. stereotype
   e. confirmation bias
   f. colorblindness
   g. privilege

6. What is race? How many races are there and why do we have different skin colors?

7. What is racism, and what is the difference between active, passive, internalized, institutional, and systemic racism?

8. Define "achievement gap" and list some of the reasons for it. Be specific.

9. What is the school-to-prison pipeline and why is it called "the new Jim Crow"? List some other institutional barriers to equity and achievement.

10. What are some successful strategies for reducing prejudice, closing the achievement gap, increasing equity, and improving school climate and student learning?

Notes: _____

_____

_____

_____

_____

_____

_____

_____

_____

_____

_____

_____

_____

_____

_____

_____

_____

_____

_____

_____

_____

_____

Culturally Responsive Teaching in This Course

Learning about the Students
- ❖ Personal posters
- ❖ Group list of things in common
- ❖ Our inner gems
- ❖ Link ups
- ❖ Culture corners activity
- ❖ Hopes, questions, concerns
- ❖ Class map of origins
- ❖ Our cultural objects
- ❖ Walk left or right
- ❖ Personal race stories
- ❖ Group discussions

Building Community
- ❖ Room arrangement
- ❖ Ground rules
- ❖ Warm-up activities
- ❖ Group discussions
- ❖ Jigsaw readings
- ❖ Food

Subject-Matter Integration
- ❖ Math: exponential ancestry
- ❖ Science: race, genetics, skin color
- ❖ Language: vocabulary, power of words
- ❖ Social Studies: Shadow of Hate video
- ❖ Music: row your boat, chord demo
- ❖ Arts: course summary

Learning about Other Cultures & Life Experiences
- ❖ Guest speakers
- ❖ Our cultural objects
- ❖ Videos: El Norte, Winona, etc.
- ❖ Readings
- ❖ Quotations

Teaching to Different Learning Styles
- ❖ PowerPoint lectures
- ❖ Worksheets & quizzes
- ❖ Group discussions
- ❖ Jigsaw readings
- ❖ Stereotype post-it activity
- ❖ Personal stories
- ❖ Guest speakers
- ❖ Eye-contact demo
- ❖ Exponential ancestry
- ❖ Skits and role plays
- ❖ Paper PPT group review
- ❖ Human graph
- ❖ Culture corners
- ❖ Art activities
- ❖ Singing
- ❖ Videos

Multiple Perspectives & Authentic Voices
- ❖ Bus accident role play
- ❖ Columbus book titles
- ❖ What's wrong with this picture?
- ❖ Name Power article
- ❖ Guest speakers
- ❖ Videos: Winona, PR Mambo
- ❖ Brother Eagle, Sister Sky
- ❖ Sitting Bull activity

Examining Our Own Attitudes
- ❖ Our race stories
- ❖ Culture corners
- ❖ We the People continuum
- ❖ Class discussions
- ❖ True-false quizzes
- ❖ Worksheets

Notes: _____

_____

_____

_____

_____

_____

_____

_____

_____

_____

_____

_____

_____

_____

_____

_____

_____

_____

_____

_____

_____

_____

_____

_____

MULTICULTURAL EDUCATION CHECKLIST © Randie Gottlieb, Ed.D.

Yes ←→ No

#	Item	Yes		No
1.	School leadership is committed to diversity and inclusion.			
2.	School policies reflect support for diversity and inclusion.			
3.	The total school culture is welcoming, inclusive and multicultural.			
4.	The school is viewed as an inclusive organization by staff, students, parents, community, and prospective hires.			
5.	The school has a comprehensive long-range diversity plan with benchmarks to measure progress.			
6.	The plan is communicated to all stakeholders on an ongoing basis.			
7.	The school has a diversity team charged with implementing the plan.			
8.	The school staff reflects the diversity in the local community.			
9.	The staff participates in ongoing, systematic diversity training.			
10.	The staff holds high expectations for students of all backgrounds, and staff behaviors reflect sensitivity to and appreciation for diversity.			
11.	There is an in-house diversity resource center available to all staff.			
12.	The school has examined its policies and programs to see if they have a disproportionate impact on some groups.			
13.	A needs assessment has been done to identify diversity issues on campus.			
14.	The curriculum acknowledges the contributions of diverse groups and helps students to see events and concepts from multiple perspectives.			

Yes ←→ No

#	Item	Yes		No
15.	Classroom instruction addresses multiple intelligences and a variety of learning styles.			
16.	Teachers use the cultural knowledge and experiences of diverse students to make learning more relevant and effective.			
17.	Instructional materials reflect diversity and are critically examined for bias.			
18.	Testing and evaluation procedures are equitable for all students.			
19.	Students are encouraged and empowered to work for social justice.			
20.	The counseling program is equitable and addresses the needs of diverse students.			
21.	The school encourages students in the use of their native language.			
22.	Physical education, music, art and other school activities reflect diversity and inclusion.			
23.	Campus clubs and extracurricular activities reflect the diversity of the student body.			
24.	Bulletin boards and other displays reflect diversity, as well as unity in diversity.			
25.	School assemblies, holidays and community activities reflect diversity.			
26.	School lunches reflect diversity.			
27.	The school works to build bridges between home, school and community.			
28.	Newsletters and other communications home reflect diversity and take the parents' language into account.			
29.	Parents from diverse groups are involved in planning, and attend school activities.			
30.				

Notes: _____

_____

_____

_____

_____

_____

_____

_____

_____

_____

_____

_____

_____

_____

_____

_____

_____

_____

_____

_____

_____

DIVERSITY & INCLUSION CHECKLIST
For Higher Education, Business & Community Groups

© Randie Gottlieb, UnityWorks Foundation, www.unityworks.org

Organization name: _____ Contact: _____ Date: _____

Core diversity values: _____

#	Item	Yes	No
ORGANIZATIONAL VALUES			
1.	Our top leadership is committed to diversity and inclusion.		
2.	We have a Board statement on diversity.		
3.	Our core values (vision, mission, policies) reflect support for diversity and inclusion.		
4.	Our personnel value diversity and inclusion.		
ORGANIZATIONAL DIVERSITY			
5.	Our board is diverse.		
6.	Our administrative personnel are diverse.		
7.	Our professional employees are diverse.		
8.	Our interns and volunteers are diverse.		
DIVERSITY GOALS AND PLANS			
9.	We have identified baseline demographics and attitudes within the organization.		
10.	We have a strategic long-range diversity plan with benchmarks to measure progress.		
11.	We have a short-range action plan with specific objectives tied to our long-range goals.		
12.	We have a diversity team charged with implementing the plan.		
13.	The plan is clearly communicated to all stakeholders on an ongoing basis.		
14.	We provide opportunities for ongoing evaluation and adjustment of the plan.		
DIVERSITY AND INCLUSION IN PRACTICE			
15.	Our products and services reflect diversity.		
16.	Our signs, displays, newsletters and marketing materials reflect diversity and inclusion.		
17.	Our customer base is becoming more diverse.		
18.	We are reaching our intended customers.		
19.	A needs assessment has been done to identify diversity issues and barriers, including whether our policies and programs have a disproportionate impact on some groups.		
20.	We have an in-house diversity resource center.		
21.	Our staff receives ongoing diversity training.		
22.	We are viewed as an inclusive organization by staff, the community, and prospective hires.		
COMMUNITY OUTREACH			
23.	We proactively engage with diverse groups in our community.		
24.	We advertise in publications that reach beyond our traditional stakeholders.		
25.	We have special events and other initiatives designed to reach underrepresented groups.		
RECRUITMENT AND RETENTION			
26.	Our recruitment policy includes diversity goals.		
27.	We have a diverse search committee.		
28.	Job openings are advertised where they will reach underrepresented groups.		
29.	We have a diverse and talented applicant pool.		
30.	We provide mentoring and other support in order to retain a diverse workforce.		

Notes: _____

_____

_____

_____

_____

_____

_____

_____

_____

_____

_____

_____

_____

_____

_____

_____

_____

_____

_____

_____

_____

_____

Diversity Action
Planning Toolkit*

* Also see pages 127, 157 and 159 for multicultural approaches and checklists

Stages of Organizational Development
From a Closed, Exclusive Organization to a Truly Multicultural One
Adapted from a conference presentation by Bailey Jackson and Evangelina Holvino

STAGE 1 **Exclusive Club**	One group is dominant and deliberately keeps others out.
STAGE 2 **The Establishment**	Hires a few token others for cosmetic reasons, but maintains the dominance of those who have traditionally held power.
STAGE 3 **Affirmative Action**	Actively recruits people from under-represented groups to comply with the law, but does not change the structure or culture of the organization. New hires often feel unwelcome and turnover is high.
STAGE 4 **Re-Examining Transforming**	Examines organizational policies, practices, structures and culture to assess their impact, and works to ensure that everyone has a fair opportunity to participate and contribute.
STAGE 5 **Diverse & Inclusive**	Everyone feels welcome and respected. Different talents, cultural strengths, perspectives and experiences are valued. People from various backgrounds are influential in organizational decision-making.

EdCHANGE
Reforming Ourselves
Transforming Our World

Stages of Multicultural School Transformation

by Paul C. Gorski (gorski@earthlink.net) for EdChange and the *Multicultural Pavilion*.
www.edchange.org & www.edchange.org/multicultural. Used with permission.

Status Quo
Traditional educational practices are maintained with no critique of existing inequities in any aspect of the school or the education system. Curricula, pedagogies, counseling practices, and all other aspects of education continue to reflect primarily white, male, upper middle class, Christian, and other privileged perspectives and approaches.

Heroes and Holidays (Food, Festivals, & Fun)
Small changes to curricula or classroom materials focus exclusively on surface-level cultural traits, often based on generalizations or stereotypes. Multicultural education is practiced as an international food fair or a celebration of a particular representative of a group. Students make headdresses or tomahawks to learn about Native American culture. Teachers purchase and display a poster of a famous woman or African American figure (usually during the paralleling history "month").

Intercultural Teaching and Learning (Cultural Dictionary)
Teachers study the customs and behaviors of the cultures from which their students come in an attempt to better understand how they should treat those students. They may have a handbook that describes how they should relate to African American students, Latino students, Asian American students, Native American students, and other groups based on an interpretation of the traditions and communication styles of those particular groups.

Human Relations (Why-Can't-We-All-Just-Get-Along)
Members of the school community are encouraged to celebrate differences by making connections across various group identities. Teachers show an enthusiasm for learning about "other" cultures beyond the Intercultural Teaching and Learning approach, drawing on the personal experiences of students so that the students learn from each other. Diversity is seen as an asset that enriches the classroom experience.

Selective Multicultural Education (We Did Multicultural Education LAST Month)
Recognizing the inequities in various aspects of education and the need to address them, teachers and administrators initiate one-time or temporary programs. They might call together a town meeting to discuss racial conflict or hire a consultant to help teachers diversify curricula. They might create a program to encourage girls to pursue math and science interests. This approach is usually reactive—in response to a particular issue or critique that has become public.

Transformative Multicultural Education (Social Justice and Equity Education)
All education practice begins with a determination to make all aspects of schools and schooling equitable and to ensure that all students have the opportunity to reach their full potential as learners. All educational practices that benefit white, male, upper middle class, or any group to the detriment of other groups is transformed to ensure equity.

Multicultural Education

Position Paper by the National Association for Multicultural Education (NAME)

* * * * *

Multicultural education is a philosophical concept built on the ideals of freedom, justice, equality, equity and human dignity as acknowledged in various documents, such as the U.S. Declaration of Independence, constitutions of South Africa and the United States, and the Universal Declaration of Human Rights adopted by the United Nations. It affirms our need to prepare student for their responsibilities in an interdependent world. It recognizes the role schools can play in developing the attitudes and values necessary for a democratic society. It values cultural differences and affirms the pluralism that students, their communities, and teachers reflect. It challenges all forms of discrimination in schools and society through the promotion of democratic principles of social justice.

Multicultural education is a process that permeates all aspects of school practices, policies and organization as a means to ensure the highest levels of academic achievement for all students. It helps students develop a positive self-concept by providing knowledge about the histories, cultures and contributions of diverse groups. It prepares all students to work actively toward structural equality in organizations and institutions by providing the knowledge, dispositions and skills for the redistribution of power and income among diverse groups. Thus, school curriculum must directly address issues of racism, sexism, classism, linguicism, ableism, ageism, heterosexism, religious intolerance and xenophobia.

Multicultural education advocates the belief that students and their life histories and experiences should be placed at the center of the teaching and learning process and that pedagogy should occur in a context that is familiar to students and that addresses multiple ways of thinking. In addition, teachers and students must critically analyze oppression and power relations in their communities, society and the world.

To accomplish these goals, multicultural education demands a school staff that is culturally competent, and to the greatest extent possible racially, culturally and linguistically diverse. Staff must be multiculturally literate and capable of including and embracing families and communities to create an environment that is supportive of multiple perspectives, experiences, and democracy. Multicultural education requires comprehensive school reform as multicultural education must pervade all aspects of the school community and organization.

Recognizing that equality and equity are not the same thing, multicultural education attempts to offer all students an equitable educational opportunity, while at the same time, encouraging students to critique society in the interest of social justice.

NAME is the leading national and international organization in the area of multicultural education. Contact NAME at name@nameorg.org or visit the website at www.nameorg.org.

"But, there's no time..."

© Randie Gottlieb, Ed.D.

> **When the curriculum is scripted, the textbooks have been chosen, and the school day is already full, what can teachers do to promote multicultural education?**

Personal
- Examine and work on eliminating personal biases and stereotypes.
- Strive to use more respectful, inclusive, bias-free language.
- Shift from being colorblind to color aware and prejudice free.

Instruction
- Emphasize higher-order thinking skills and more engaging curricula.*
- Vary teaching styles to reach students with diverse learning styles.
- Teach students communication and consultation skills.
- Use cooperative learning, peer teaching and other inclusive strategies to promote positive interactions among diverse students.
- Examine textbooks and other instructional materials for bias.
- Point out inaccuracies and missing chapters.
- Include multiple perspectives and authentic voices when possible.
- Pay attention to diversity when selecting images for bulletin boards, posters, etc.
- Teach students to ask critical questions and to investigate truth.
- Differentiate instruction and assessment to provide equitable rather than exactly equal opportunities for learning.
- Be thoughtful when assigning homework, recognizing that some students do not have access to computers, the internet or other resources.

Classroom Interactions
- Cultivate a safe classroom environment where students feel free to express themselves honestly.
- Hold high expectations for all students, looking beyond a single standardized test score.
- Notice who tends to get called on and encouraged during class, and strive for greater equity.
- Avoid assigning classroom tasks by gender, e.g., boys as team leaders, girls as notetakers.
- Have extra coats, school supplies and snacks available, and distribute them quietly if needed.

School Climate and Advocacy
- Foster conversations with colleagues about ways to promote equity in school.
- Advocate to keep low-income, ELL and students of color from being placed unfairly into lower academic tracks, and to be admitted to higher-level programs when appropriate.
- Speak out against bias in school policies and practices, including discriminatory discipline.
- Share models of unity in diversity to serve as examples and inspiration for others.
- Investigate and promote programs with a track record of success in helping all students learn.
- Volunteer to serve on the school's diversity team and to assist with its action plan.

---

* For example, see "Engaging Curriculum: A Foundation for Positive School Culture" by David Hunter <www.ascd.org/ascd-express/vol9/910-hunter.aspx>.

UnityWorks K-12 School Programs and Activities*

UnityWorks empowers the site team at each school to design and implement its own blueprint for change. Teams have planned a wide variety of multicultural activities and programs including:

Awareness and Training

1. Held an orientation on diversity and acceptance for all new students.
2. Conducted a school climate survey involving staff, students and parents.
3. Organized school-wide professional development based on UnityWorks training activities.
4. Trained teachers on how to work more effectively with English language learners.
5. Trained student leaders in peer mediation and conflict-resolution techniques.
6. Purchased multicultural books and videos for the school resource library.
7. Established the "UnityWorks Minute" where at each staff meeting, one teacher is asked to share an activity s/he has done with their students to promote unity.

Classroom Activities

1. Led classroom discussions on stereotyping and prejudice.
2. Revised lesson plans to include authentic voices and multiple perspectives.
3. Developed monthly half-hour lessons on diversity for the entire student body.
4. Prepared and offered UnityWorks coupons to reward positive student behaviors.
5. The UnityWorks team, 700 students, and their teachers created self-portraits (see next page), mixing paint to accurately match their own skin colors. The portraits were then displayed throughout the school as part of a larger lesson on diversity and acceptance. As a result, incidents of racial bias, which had been increasing in recent months, stopped completely. There was also a significant drop in discipline issues and suspensions, attributed in large part to the UnityWorks program. (The activity is described in our Teaching Unity book.)

Extra-curricular and Other School Activities

1. Established a student multicultural club that has studied different cultures, learned about Islam at the local mosque, visited homeless children, and organized a winter clothing drive.
2. Posted photos of students with a world map showing their countries of origin.
3. Organized an exhibit on African-American history for the entire school.
4. Displayed multicultural artwork by students and by artists from around the world.
5. Hosted an essay competition and a poetry slam on the theme of unity in diversity.
6. Scheduled school assemblies with speakers on a variety of multicultural topics.
7. Brought in a play on the Japanese internment to share the story of one American family's experience during World War II. After the show, the actors engendered a lively discussion by asking the audience: Why were people forcibly removed from their homes and imprisoned? Do you think this could happen today? What can we do to help prevent it?
8. Organized a series of traditional activities (native drumming and dancing, basketry, root digging, storytelling and moccasin making) based on the understanding that people can learn to respect other cultures when they first respect their own.

* For more detailed descriptions, visit our website and click on Programs > Overview > Sample School Activities. Some activities were organized through the EMPIRE Program, which was the precursor to UnityWorks.

Community Outreach

1. Put the school reader board in English and Spanish to increase parent engagement.
2. Sponsored community service projects designed by students and community members.
3. Participated in the national Stand Against Racism campaign organized by the YWCA.
4. Encouraged parent involvement through family nights and cultural activities.

Partnerships and Collaborative Projects

1. Five high schools collaborated to produce student-written plays on prejudice, stereotyping and gangs, and performed them for large audiences of parents and community members.
2. Established the InterValley Ambassadors student exchange program to increase understanding and acceptance of youth from different ethnic neighborhoods.
3. High school students developed and taught lessons to elementary students about bullying.
4. One middle school partnered with a high school on an arts program, including a youth orchestra and an Art Board Project highlighting authors and artists from around the world, with biographies written in English and Spanish to support students' bilingual skills.
5. A high school partnered with an elementary school, with older students helping younger ones to learn about our human family by researching and presenting information on various countries. Topics included history, geography, climate, religion, music, dance, art, architecture, culture, language, customs, food, sports, traditional clothing and more.

Cultural Performances and Celebrations

1. Arranged for performers from diverse ethnic backgrounds, for example, a Lakota hoop dancer whose presentation was designed to convey the concept of unity in diversity.
2. Organized a multicultural festival on the theme of "Celebrating Our Differences," after months of planning involving the entire school. Teams of teachers, students, staff and parents researched the diverse cultures in the local community, and each developed a presentation that included traditional dances, food, music, crafts and other elements of their culture. The goal was to increase parent involvement, which went from only five people at the start of the project to over 450 at the culminating event. The teams are now creating a multicultural recipe book, with each recipe accompanied by an explanation of the significance of the food to that culture.
3. Hosted a "World Cultural Night" with displays designed to showcase the home countries of the international exchange students. Community members enjoyed speaking with the students, and received stickers in their "passports" for each "country" visited.

Evaluating Multicultural Activities

© Randie Gottlieb, Ed.D.

Program or Activity: _____

SOME ITEMS TO CONSIDER*

CONTENT		Yes	No	Comments
1	The activity is developmentally appropriate.			
2	The content is complete, accurate and unbiased.			
3	It presents multiple perspectives.			
4	It includes authentic voices.			
5	It helps students to learn about other cultures.			
6	It helps students to learn about their own culture.			
7	It acknowledges similarities and differences.			
8	It challenges prejudice and stereotypes.			
METHODS				
9	It draws on student voices, interests and experiences.			
10	It encourages students to think critically.			
11	It encourages group problem solving.			
12	Teaching methods address diverse learning styles.			
ATTITUDES, VALUES, OUTCOMES				
13	It promotes self-awareness.			
14	It promotes understanding, cooperation and respect.			
15	It builds positive relationships among diverse groups.			
16	It provides opportunities for service to others.			
17	It encourages students to work for social justice.			
PLANNING and PROCESS				
18	Diverse stakeholders are involved in planning the activity.			
19	Parents and community members are included.			
20	Feedback is welcomed and incorporated in future planning.			

* Not all items will be relevant to every program or activity.

Notes: _____

_____

_____

_____

_____

_____

Dominant and Subordinate Groups © Randie Gottlieb, Ed.D.

People have divided our human family into "us" and "them." Perhaps most obvious are the borders dividing one nation from another, but we have also created mental boundaries that divide us, reinforce hierarchies, and push "others" to the margins: Whites over Blacks, rich over poor, males over females. Since borders have been constructed by people, we can also dismantle them. This takes courage, but we can reach across those lines of difference to find unity in our diversity. We can create a new sense of community based on equity, inclusion and respect. We might begin by identifying the "borders" within our own workplaces, communities and schools. Fill in the table below by identifying the dominant and subordinate (or marginalized) groups in your own organization.

Some Types of Diversity		In Groups	Out Groups
1	Race		
2	Gender		
3	Age		
4	Ethnicity		
5	Ability		
6	Nationality		
7	Language		
8	Culture		
9	Religion		
10	Education		
11	Economic class		
12	Physical appearance		
13	Sexuality		
14	Family structure		
15	Work		
16			

Is My Classroom Inclusive?

Ref: Sapon-Shevin, *Because We Can Change the World. Used with permission.*

1. How would your students describe their classroom?

2. Do the students know each other?

3. Do they know how to ask respectful questions about their differences?

4. Do they interact comfortably with a wide range of other students?

5. Do they know how to include classmates with challenging behaviors, different languages, learning styles or disabilities?

6. When a student needs help, does s/he feel free to ask another student?

7. How do students respond to another student's accomplishment?

8. Are there ways for students and teachers to easily bring up concerns?

9. What happens when a conflict arises?

10. Do students know how to respond when someone is confused, hurt, scared?

11. Do they challenge discriminatory or stereotypical remarks, and actively work to include those who have been excluded?

Making Students Feel Welcome at School
© Randie Gottlieb, Ed.D.

Establish a relationship
- Build a personal relationship with difficult students.
- Greet them as they get off the bus or enter the classroom.
- Seat them close to you, pronounce their names correctly, smile at them.
- Spend time with them outside of class (attend their soccer game or band performance, etc.).
- Select a particularly difficult student for special attention, e.g. show several staff his/her photo and ask them to smile and say "Hello, Eric" at every opportunity.

Teach and model respect
- Treat kids with respect to earn their respect.
- Insist on courtesy and fairness in and outside of class.
- Teach direct lessons about prejudice and discrimination.
- Allow zero tolerance for bias (no racial slurs or sexist jokes).
- Discipline students fairly, not based on their color, gender, reputation, etc.

Create an inclusive classroom
- Construct classroom rules together as a group.
- Increase your own knowledge of the diverse cultures in your room.
- Include multiple perspectives and authentic voices in your lesson plans.
- Make sure females and people of color are readily visible in your texts, posters and videos.
- Review all instructional materials for stereotyping and bias.
- Make learning interesting and culturally relevant.
- Teach to different learning styles and include cooperative learning strategies.
- Put up a changing photo display of students at work, so they can see themselves as positive members of the class.

Create high expectations
- Call students to a higher standard and offer the support needed to reach that standard.
- Teach them the hidden rules of school so they know how to succeed.
- Ask each student what s/he needs to be successful in your class.

Listen well
- Create a safe space for listening: morning circle, written suggestion box, quiet corner, etc.
- Listen to students even if you don't agree with them.
- Use phrases like: What did you mean? How do you feel about that? Tell me more.
- Role play problem situations with teacher and student switching roles.
- Teach consultation and conflict resolution skills.

Boost student esteem
- Put resistant students in charge of tasks that will make them look important in front of peers.
- Use peer teaching to give all students an opportunity to show that they are good at something.
- Provide students with opportunities for service to others.
- If criticism is necessary, sandwich it between positive feedback or praise.
- Give students plenty of encouragement, and send home positive notes.

Are More Teachers of Color Required to Effectively Reach Students of Color?

© Randie Gottlieb, Ed.D.

Yes and no. While students of color make up over half of the public school population, teachers of color are only 18% of the teaching force, meaning that over 80% of school teachers are white. With a more diverse staff, more students would have role models, and the opportunity to see their own reality reflected and validated in the school setting. [1, 2, 3, 4]

Recent research highlights the unique role that teachers of color can play in improving educational experiences and outcomes for students of color.[5] Some studies have shown improved attendance and academic achievement for such students when they have teachers from the same race or cultural background. Students of color also perceive those teachers as being more accessible, caring and engaging. In addition, teachers of color are more likely to remain in high needs schools longer than white teachers, thereby adding essential stability and professional competence.

A diverse staff would also allow white students to see from new perspectives and to avoid some of the blind spots of the traditional curriculum. "It's important for our social fabric, for our sense as a nation, that students are engaging with people who think, talk, and act differently than them," says Kevin Gilbert of the National Education Association.[6] For a more balanced education, all students need "mirrors" as well as "windows" on the world.

It would also be naïve to think that *only* teachers of color can be effective in reaching students of color, or that *all* teachers of color are necessarily good teachers. By claiming that we must wait until more such teachers are hired, white teachers and administrators abdicate their own responsibilities. Teachers of all colors and backgrounds can learn to be culturally responsive.

> Hiring more teachers of color is not necessarily the answer to the problem, for most of them received their professional training in White-dominated university schools of education…They have been trained to carry out the directives of White-created curricula, to uphold the standards geared for the middle-class White child…and there's always the fear of losing their jobs if they stray from the White-dominated administration's educational patterns and policies. To make an impression on their bosses, some teachers of color will try to outdo their White colleagues in making students of color toe the traditional educational line.
> —**Nathan Rutstein**, *The Racial Conditioning of Our Children*, p.22

References
1. www.americanprogress.org/issues/education-k-12/reports/2017/09/14/437667/america-needs-teachers-color-selective-teaching-profession
2. www.americanprogress.org/issues/race/report/2014/05/04/88962/teacher-diversity-revisited
3. http://nces.ed.gov/pubs2013/2013314.pdf
4. www.theatlantic.com/education/archive/2015/08/teachers-of-color-white-students/400553
5. www.nea.org/home/65429.htm
6. https://newpittsburghcourieronline.com/2014/05/04/us-teachers-nowhere-as-diverse-as-their-students

What Can Teachers Do?

Ways to reduce prejudice and create more inclusive classrooms

© Randie Gottlieb, Ed.D.

For Ourselves

1. Model acceptance of and appreciation for differences.
2. Build a safe, inclusive, welcoming and respectful classroom community.
3. Interrupt biased remarks and behaviors rather than ignoring them.
4. Understand the relationship between teacher expectations and student achievement.
5. Become more aware of our own prejudices and our interactions with students.
6. Learn to teach in multicultural settings and to deal with feelings of rejection and superiority.

Curriculum and Instruction

1. Provide instructional materials that are free of bias and stereotyping.
2. Include multiple perspectives, drawing on multicultural literature and authentic voices.
3. Study the contributions of different genders, racial, ethnic, religious and other groups.
4. Expose students to positive role models from diverse groups through speakers, videos, posters, field trips, pen pals, community service projects and other means.
5. Intentionally seek out and share "missing chapters" and "counternarratives" through biographies, stories, songs and images that contradict prevailing myths and stereotypes.
6. Incorporate students' languages, cultures and life experiences into the curriculum to increase motivation and as a springboard for learning.
7. Differentiate instruction by providing different avenues for learning and assessment.
8. Provide alternatives to tracking and labeling.
9. Assign a study buddy or language partner, and use peer teaching and cooperative learning.
10. Teach students how to succeed in school and offer extra help as needed.

Social Awareness and Relationship Skills

1. Encourage cross-group friendships.
2. Teach cross-cultural awareness, consultation and conflict resolution skills.
3. Practice positive discipline and restorative justice, with fair consequences for violations.
4. Teach human virtues like courtesy, generosity, service, truthfulness and courage.
5. Foster in all students a positive self-image rooted in a sense of personal dignity.
6. Teach directly about prejudice and discrimination, and encourage open discussion.
7. Let students know that noticing differences is not the same as having prejudice.
8. Encourage and empower students to work for social justice.
9. Teach them about the oneness of humanity, the value of diversity, and the need for unity.
10. Let them know you care.

What Can Our Organization Do?

© Randie Gottlieb, Ed.D.

Hiring people of color is not enough. Creating individual awareness is not enough. Adding the word "diversity" to our mission statement is not enough.

> **We need to create a comprehensive, systematic strategy for change. It's an investment that takes time, resources and strong leadership.**

1. Provide everyone in the organization with systematic, comprehensive and ongoing diversity training, including an awareness of personal attitudes and behaviors.

2. Examine every aspect of the organization (vision, mission, culture, policies, recruiting, hiring, promotions, evaluations, incentives, informal mentoring and support systems) and systematically remove all barriers that favor one group or discriminate against another.

3. Change power relationships from a top-down hierarchy to a more inclusive framework.

4. Encourage dialogue and active listening, even if dominant groups are uncomfortable or insist there is no problem.

5. Use focus groups to identify key issues and concerns.

6. Create opportunities for people of diverse backgrounds to work together.

7. Establish mentoring programs (internal) and partnerships (external) with diverse groups.

8. Create inclusive policies, e.g., flextime, on-site day care, pa/maternity leave, job sharing.

9. Show that diversity is valued by not trying to make everyone the same.

10. Regularly communicate the institution's commitment to diversity through meetings, publications, displays, newsletters, social media, press releases and other means.

11. Identify and publicize models of unity in diversity.

12. When planning community outreach and marketing, pay attention to staff attitudes and behaviors, communication styles, language, dress, culturally appropriate strategies, reception areas, visual images, background music, wall displays, etc.

13. Insist on zero tolerance for sexual harassment, racist jokes and inappropriate pictures.

14. Hold staff and faculty accountable for their behavior through rewards and sanctions.

15. Create structures and processes that will support change efforts, e.g., a diversity council, incentive programs, and a mandatory orientation for new employees.

16. Start with one department that can serve as an example for the others.

17. Persevere in the face of active resistance and the power of the status quo.

Creating a Successful Diversity Action Plan

© Randie Gottlieb, Ed.D.

Diversity Represents Opportunity

Diversity is not just another fad. Our nation's demographics are changing, and our educational institutions face a growing number of pressing diversity issues. We can deny that these issues exist and oppose the necessary changes, or welcome this opportunity for growth.

Diversity is not about condemning white males, giving unfair advantages to special groups, or implementing mandatory programs as a cosmetic response to discrimination complaints. Rather, it's about creating a respectful and inclusive environment where everyone feels welcome and can make a valuable contribution. It means removing obstacles to advancement for qualified people of diverse backgrounds. It results in improved morale, decreased absenteeism and turnover, greater creativity, and increased productivity through the utilization of diverse talents, experiences and perspectives. It's a responsibility that belongs not just to the human resource department, but to all of us.

Essential Components of a Successful Diversity Plan

1. Committed leadership from within the organization.
2. A clear vision of where we want to be, with a good idea of where we are now.
3. Specific, phased and measurable goals with a step-by-step plan for achieving them.
4. A knowledgeable team in charge of developing, communicating and implementing the plan.
5. A timely implementation strategy with benchmarks for measuring progress.
6. A learning community to provide networking, sharing of best practices, and ongoing support.

In addition to the creation of organizational structures that promote equity and that support sustainable positive change, an effective diversity plan may include systematic staff training that combines personal awareness with practical knowledge and skills. Rather than asking the diversity team to implement a series of directives from above, a grassroots approach increases buy-in by empowering teams to design and implement their own agendas for change.

Committed Leadership

An effective diversity plan needs one or more leaders from within the organization who are committed for the short, medium and long term. These are not just the check signers, but the cheerleaders and champions of the diversity effort. They should be out in front, accessible, asking the hard questions, and holding people accountable.

Recognizing Diversity Issues

A diversity issue exists when any policy, practice or structure has a disproportionate impact on a particular group. For example, are women and people of color largely absent from administrative positions? Are certain groups of students over- or underrepresented in special education, remedial or gifted programs? Are there disproportionate levels of academic achievement, discipline referrals, suspensions or expulsions for certain groups, and if so, why? Perceptions are also important. Do staff, students, community members and prospective hires see your school, district or university as an inclusive organization? Issues must first be identified in order to address them effectively.

Identifying Needs

A needs assessment can provide concrete direction for a long-range diversity plan and establish a baseline from which to measure future progress. Data can be gathered through personal interviews, surveys and focus groups. Asking each group the same questions allows for comparison of results. Look for patterns. There may be differing responses among schools, between teachers and students, males and females, or by those from different income levels or ethnic backgrounds. The UnityWorks School Climate Survey can be a useful assessment tool.

Sample Diversity Goals

1. Develop an inclusive vision and mission statement for our organization.
2. Create a respectful, welcoming and inclusive campus culture.
3. Diversify campus leadership, advisory boards and mid-level management.
4. Recruit and retain a diverse workforce and provide systematic diversity training.
5. Recruit and retain a diverse student body.
6. Incorporate multicultural and global perspectives into the curriculum.
7. Practice culturally-responsive, anti-bias teaching in all subjects and departments.
8. Increase graduation rates for underrepresented and underserved groups.
9. Reduce disproportionate discipline referrals, suspensions and expulsions.
10. Forge strategic diversity partnerships with alumni, local businesses and the community.

Communicating the Plan

Once your organization has adopted a diversity plan, it should be shared with all stakeholders on an ongoing basis. For example, in a K-12 setting, the plan can be included on a district web site and on school bulletin boards. It can be communicated to students during an all-school assembly. Information can be sent home to parents, and a short video can be played during open houses and parent-teacher conferences. A brochure can be developed for new employees and reviewed during staff meetings.

In a college or university setting, the goals can be publicized to prospective students, staff and faculty, and used to build internal culture as well as external awareness among alumni, donors and the wider community. This effort can be part of an integrated marketing and communications plan utilizing displays, websites, social media, direct mail, print publications, information tables, bus posters, reader boards, sponsorships, radio and TV advertising, and other means.

Implementing the Plan

Translating vision into action requires persistence, encouragement and a commitment to learning and improvement. It is often better to begin with small steps and to grow organically through an ongoing process of consultation, action and reflection.

At its first meeting, for example, the diversity team might draft a long-range organizational vision and identify one or more priorities for the next 3-6 months. In setting its initial goals, the team will want to prepare a timeline of activities and decide who will carry them out. They should also take into account the perspectives of and impact on various stakeholders, potential challenges and opportunities, spheres of greatest influence, and available human and material resources. The materials included with this packet can serve as useful tools for creating an effective organizational plan.

Team Visioning Exercise

This exercise can be done with your UnityWorks team or as a series of focus groups with different stakeholders in your organization. For example, a school site team can invite groups of students, parents, teachers, administrators, or community members to participate in the following activity.

How might our school be different if English language learners, low-income students, or students of color and their families had input into:

❖ The curriculum
❖ Teaching methods
❖ Instructional materials
❖ Assessments
❖ School rules

❖ Discipline policies
❖ Daily schedule
❖ Facility design
❖ Teacher selection and training
❖ Other topics?

1. Brainstorm as a group to address one or more of the topics listed above.
2. Consider practical recommendations, and also take a few minutes to come up with some creative "out-of-the-box" ideas.
3. Come to a consensus and then prioritize your recommendations.
4. Use images and/or text to illustrate your ideas on the chart paper.
5. Be prepared to give a 2-3 minute presentation to the larger group.

Notes: _____

_____

_____

_____

_____

RESEARCH DEPT. _____

_____

_____

Multicultural Web Resources

All websites are correct at the time of printing.

Addressing Student Diversity: Comprehensive list of web resources on all aspects of diversity.
< www.mhhe.com/socscience/education/diverse.mhtml#addressing >

Awesome Library: www.awesomelibrary.org/Classroom/Social_Studies/Multicultural/Multicultural.html

Center for the Study of White American Culture: A multiracial organization that supports self-discovery among white Americans and encourages dialogue among all racial and cultural groups.
< www.euroamerican.org >

Diversity Links: Extensive links to online diversity resources.
< http://web.archive.org/web/20040207065447/www.wesleyan.edu/psyc/list.html >

Diversity Store: Banners, buttons, flags, magnets, posters and more. < www.diversitystore.com >

Education Week: "The Web's authoritative source on K-12 education." < www.edweek.org >

Educational Resources Information Center (ERIC): "The world's premier database of journal and non-journal education literature." < www.eric.ed.gov >

Edutopia: < www.edutopia.org/blog/preparing-cultural-diversity-resources-teachers >

Gender Spectrum: Resources for gender and transgender topics. < www.genderspectrum.org >

Government Alliance on Racial Equity: Training, tools, resources. < www.racialequityalliance.org >

Guide to Being an Anti-Racism Activist: At the individual, community and national levels.
< thoughtco.com/things-you-can-do-to-help-end-racism-3026187 >

Implicit Attitude Test: Test yourself for hidden biases. < www.tolerance.org/hidden_bias/index.html >

Intercultural Press: Online bookstore. < https://openlibrary.org/publishers/Intercultural_Press >

Multicultural Lesson Plans and Resources: < www.cloudnet.com/~edrbsass/edmulticult.htm >

Multicultural Pavilion: Articles, lesson plans, workshops, teacher resources, case studies, handouts, speeches, songs, multicultural links: < www.edchange.org > and < www.edchange.org/multicultural >. For film reviews: < www.edchange.org/multicultural/filmreviews.html >

National Association for Multicultural Education: NAME provides leadership in equity, diversity and multicultural education, from preschool through higher education. < www.nameorg.org >

National Center for Transgender Equality: https://transequality.org/school-action-center

National Education Association:
< www.nea.org/tools/resources-addressing-multicultural-diversity-issues-in-your-classroom.htm >

Race – The Power of an Illusion: 3-hour video series by California Newsreel with links to additional resources and lesson plans. < http://newsreel.org/video/race-the-power-of-an-illusion >

Race Forward: Research and training on racial justice. < www.raceforward.org >

Race Relations: Articles, resources, forums. < http://racerelations.about.com >

Social Justice Books: Excellent selection of multicultural and social justice books for children, young adults and educators. **<** socialjusticebooks.org >

Society for Intercultural Education, Training and Research:
"The world's largest interdisciplinary network for students and professionals working in the field of intercultural communication."
< www.sietarusa.org >

Teaching for Change: Teacher resources, books, articles for teaching social justice. < www.TeachingForChange.org >

Teaching Tolerance: A wealth of online resources to support anti-bias activism in every venue of American life. < www.tolerance.org >

Understanding Race: History—Human Variation—Lived Experience. A Project of the American Anthropological Association. < www.understandingrace.org >

UnityWorks Foundation: Promoting the oneness of humanity through diversity training, resources and support for schools, colleges and community groups. < www.unityworks.org >

U.S. Department of Education: National goals, programs, grants. < www.ed.gov/diversity-opportunity >

Some Resources on Poverty

Association for Supervision and Curriculum Development:
< www.ascd.org > click on Books/Pub > Poverty

Center on Urban Poverty and Social Change: < http://povertycenter.cwru.edu >

Children's Defense Fund: < http://childrensdefense.org >

Institute on Poverty: < www.ssc.wisc.edu/irp >

Institute on Race and Poverty: < www.irpumn.org/website >

Kids Can Make a Difference: < www.kidscanmakeadifference.org >

Make Poverty History: < www.makepovertyhistory.org/schools/index.shtml >

National Law Center on Homelessness and Poverty: < www.nlchp.org >

Poverty and Race Research Action Council: < prrac.org >

Poverty Guidelines, Research & Measurement: < http://aspe.hhs.gov/poverty/index.shtml >

Poverty Lines: < http://data.worldbank.org/topic/poverty >

Poverty, Race and Inequality Program: < www.northwestern.edu/ipr/research/respoverty1.html >

PovertyNet: < www.worldbank.org/poverty >

Program on Poverty and Social Welfare Policy: < www.fordschool.umich.edu/research/poverty >

Reaching and Teaching Students in Poverty: Strategies for Erasing the Opportunity Gap, Paul Gorski. Available on < www.amazon.com >.

Teaching with Poverty in Mind: Eric Jensen, <www.ascd.org >

U.S. Census Bureau: < www.census.gov/hhes/www/poverty.html >

Notes: _____

_____

_____

_____

_____

_____

_____

_____

_____

_____

_____

_____

_____

_____

_____

_____

_____

_____

_____

_____

_____

_____

Courage

A song by Bob Blue

A small thing once happened at school
That brought up a question for me,
And somehow it forced me to see
The price that I pay to be cool.

Diane is a girl that I know.
She's strange, like she doesn't belong.
I don't mean to say that it's wrong.
We don't like to be with her, though.

And so, when we all made a plan
To have this big party at Sue's,
Most kids in the school got the news,
But no one invited Diane.

The thing about Taft Junior High
Is, secrets don't last very long.
I acted like nothing was wrong
When I saw Diane start to cry.

I know you may think that I'm cruel.
It doesn't make me very proud.
I just went along with the crowd.
It's sad, but you have to in school.

You can't pick the friends you prefer.
You fit in as well as you can.
I couldn't be friends with Diane,
'Cause then they would treat me like her.

In one class at Taft Junior High,
We study what people have done
With gas chamber, bomber, and gun
At Auschwitz, Japan, and My Lai.

I don't understand all I learn.
Sometimes I just sit there and cry.
The whole world stood idly by
To watch as the innocent burn.

Like robots obeying some rule.
Atrocities done by the mob.
All innocent, doing their job.
And what was it for? Was it cool?

The world was aware of this Hell,
But how many cried out in shame?
What heroes, and who was to blame?
A story that no one dared tell.

I promise to do what I can
To not let it happen again.
To care for all women and men.
I'll start by inviting Diane. ■

The late Bob Blue was an elementary school teacher in Wellesley, MA. "He wanted people to draw inspiration from what he had to say," says his daughter Lara Shepard-Blue, "and they have. Hundreds of people who for years have been spreading his music will continue to do so. He would like that."

Watch here: < www.youtube.com/watch?v=X6XeP3uyfiw&feature=youtu.be > sung by Kate Levin. Also < www.dannicholsmusic.com/news-feed/2012/9/27/dan-covers-courage-bob-blue-on-the-road-to-eden-tour > sung by Dan Nichols (start at .45 seconds).

Diversity Action Plan

School/Organization: _____ City: _____ Date: _____

Planning Team Members: _____

Vision Statement/Goals:

	Objective	Action Steps	Time Frame	Resources Needed	Who	Progress/Outcomes	Evidence
1							
2							
3							
4							
5							

Notes: _____

_____

_____

_____

_____

_____

_____

_____

_____

_____

_____

_____

_____

_____

_____

_____

_____

_____

_____

_____

_____

_____

_____

Individual Action Plan

Name: _____

Date: _____

School/Organization: _____

How can I make a difference?

Name at least one concrete action that you can personally take to help move us closer to the vision of equity, inclusion and unity. Include when and how you will begin.

I will: _____

_____

_____

_____

_____

Additional
Items

Multicultural Education
Key Concepts and Vocabulary

1. **Race:** An artificial classification of humankind into subgroups (e.g., Caucasoid, Mongoloid, Negroid) based on observable physical characteristics such as skin pigmentation, hair texture, facial features and bodily proportions.

2. **Culture:** The sum total of all learned patterns of thinking, feeling and doing, of a particular people at a particular time. A human group with shared language, religion, social organization, values, customs, tools, technology, symbols, music, foods, etc.

3. **Ethnic group:** A distinctive population within the larger society, with common physical and cultural characteristics, and who possess a shared history and identity.

4. **Nationality:** Identity based on one's nation of birth or citizenship.

5. **Immigrant:** Someone who moves to a new country to live.

6. **Xenophobia:** An unreasonable fear or dislike of strangers and people from other countries.

7. **Minority:** An ethnic, racial, religious or other group having a distinctive presence within a society, but with limited power or representation relative to other groups. This subordinate status rather than population size is the chief defining characteristic.

8. **Socialization:** The process of transmitting cultural norms to the next generation.

9. **Ethnocentrism:** Belief by members of one group that their culture is better than all other cultures, and that their way of doing things is correct.

10. **Assimilation:** The process of giving up most or all of one's culture to take on the ways of another, thus becoming incorporated and absorbed into the dominant group. The *melting pot*.

11. **Acculturation:** Taking on elements of a new culture without giving up one's own.

12. **Segregation:** To isolate or separate a particular group from others, e.g., the policy of creating separate facilities for Blacks and Whites during the "separate but equal" Jim Crow era.

13. **Integration:** Free association of people from different backgrounds in various social domains. Also, the intentional distribution of marginalized groups with the goal of achieving racial or gender balance in areas of education, housing, employment and other sectors of society.

14. **Cultural relativism:** Belief that all cultures are good and right within themselves, that no culture has elements that are best for all people, and that since our views are shaped by our culture, it is not possible to make meaningful judgments about the validity of another culture.

15. **Cultural pluralism:** Belief in the value of diversity, with the expectation that each group has something to contribute to the larger society. Diverse groups maintain their unique identities within a shared majority culture. Coexistence in a *salad bowl* rather than a *melting pot*.

16. **Cultural appropriation:** When members of one culture adopt cultural expressions (symbols, music, artwork, dance, speech, clothing, ceremonies) of another group; especially when those elements are misused or desecrated, even against the expressed wishes of the original culture, and when that group itself is marginalized and receives no credit or benefit therefrom.

17. **Unity in diversity:** Belief in the oneness of humanity while valuing diversity, as in the human body whose many different parts function together in harmony as one organic whole.

18. **Stereotype:** A widely-held, oversimplified, usually negative view about a particular group of people, characterizing them with regard to certain traits, qualities or behaviors.

19. **Scapegoat:** A person or group bearing blame for the misfortunes or sins of others.

20. **Prejudice:** A preconceived, irrational dislike for a particular race, religion, nationality, gender or other group, often based on stereotypes.

21. **Discrimination:** The act of treating people differently (usually negatively) based on their race, culture, religion, gender, sexual orientation, disability, etc.

22. **Racism:** A system of inequality based on race, where one group has access to better jobs, pay, housing, schools and other resources and opportunities, even if individuals from the privileged group aren't particularly powerful or overtly prejudiced.

23. **Genocide:** The systematic extermination of an entire racial, ethnic or national group.

24. **Ally:** One who is not being oppressed and chooses to stand up for those who are, e.g., a straight person who stands up for LGBT people, or a man who stands up for women's rights.

25. **Equity:** The guarantee of fair treatment, allocation of resources, and access to programs for all students, including the provision of bias-free educational settings, curriculum, and instructional methods and materials that address the learning needs of all.

26. **Interdependence:** Mutually reliant; dependent upon one another for common well-being.

27. **Multiple perspectives:** Different viewpoints about an event or idea.

28. **Culturally responsive teaching:** Educational practice that incorporates the backgrounds, learning styles and experiences of all students, to make learning more relevant and effective.

29. **Multicultural education:** Education designed to produce people with the knowledge, skills and attitudes needed to function effectively in a multicultural society. This includes teaching about and valuing diversity, including the histories, perspectives and contributions of diverse peoples.

30. **Anti-bias education:** Education that challenges all forms of prejudice and discrimination, and empowers students to work for the democratic ideals of freedom and social justice.

31. **Global education:** Interdisciplinary education focusing on global issues, perspectives, events, and relationships among countries. Includes study of human rights, the environment, economic and political systems, world history, cultures and technology.

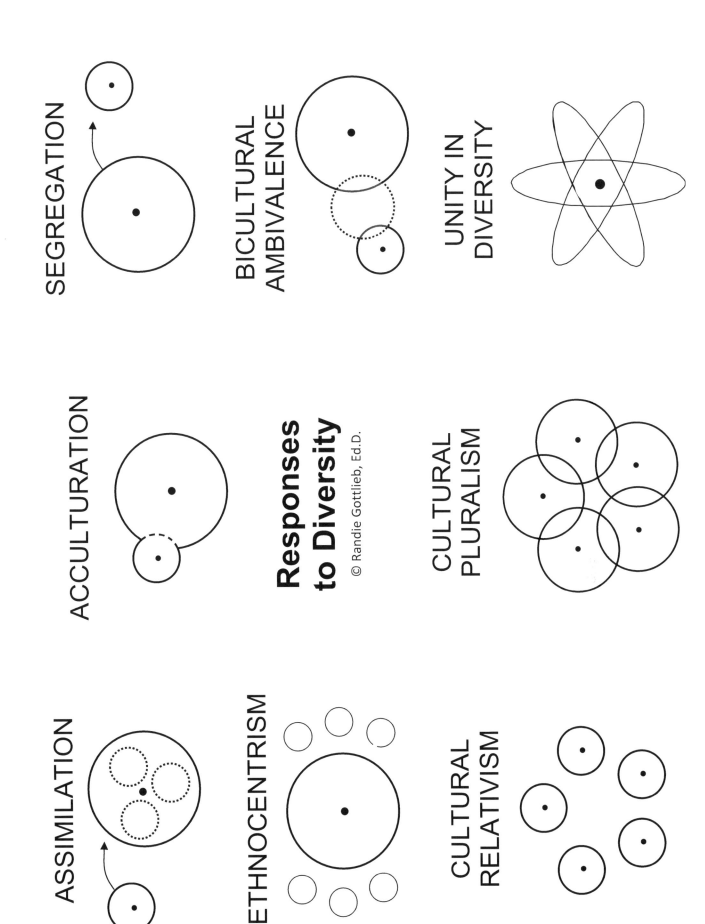

SEGREGATION

BICULTURAL AMBIVALENCE

UNITY IN DIVERSITY

ACCULTURATION

Responses to Diversity
© Randie Gottlieb, Ed.D.

CULTURAL PLURALISM

ASSIMILATION

ETHNOCENTRISM

CULTURAL RELATIVISM

Our HIStory and HERitage

1. Paul Revere
In 1775, Revere and William Dawes were sent to warn Samuel Adams and John Hancock of British plans to march from Boston to seize patriot military stores at Concord. A signal was established to warn if the British were coming by land or by sea. Along the road to Lexington, Revere warned residents that the British were coming. He was captured. (http://darter.ocps.net/classroom/revolution/revere.htm)

2. Jacques Cousteau
Underwater explorer, researcher and educator. (www.cousteau.org/en/heritage/captain/man.php)

3. Carl Sagan
Astronomer, planetary scientist and educator. (www.carlsagan.com)

4. Dr. Martin Luther King, Jr.
Civil rights activist. (www.thekingcenter.com)

5. Bill Gates
Chair and Chief Software Architect of Microsoft Corporation, and philanthropist. (www.microsoft.com/billgates/default.asp)

6. Mozart
World famous Austrian musician and composer. (en.wikipedia.org/wiki/Wolfgang_Amadeus_Mozart)

© Randie Gottlieb, Ed.D.

1. Sybil Ludington
Sixteen-year-old who, in 1777, rode twice as far as Paul Revere, nearly 40 miles in one night, to round up Revolutionary troops when British solders were attacking nearby Danbury, CT. (www.geocities.com/Heartland/Plains/1789/sybil.html)

2. Sylvia Earle
Marine biologist and oceanographer known as "Her Deepness" and "The Sturgeon General," who in 1979, walked untethered on the sea floor at a depth of 3,300 feet—lower than anyone before or since. Earle pioneered research on marine ecosystems and has led more than 50 expeditions totaling over 6,000 hours underwater. She has been an explorer-in-residence at the National Geographic Society since 1998, and was named *Time Magazine's* first "hero for the planet." (www.nationalgeographic.com/council/eir/bio_earle.html)

3. Annie Jump Cannon
Astronomer and world's expert in stellar classification. She classified the characteristics of over 350,000 stars, starting in 1896, making Carl Sagan's work possible. (www.wellesley.edu/Astronomy/annie)

4. Ella Baker
Organizer, activist and unsung hero of the U.S. Civil Rights movement. She co-founded the powerful Southern Christian Leadership Conference with MLK, and devoted six decades of her life to over 50 social justice organizations. (www.ellabakercenter.org)

5. Grace Murray Hopper
A leader in computer software design, Rear Admiral Dr. Grace Murray Hopper helped develop the first commercial computer, invented the compiler (the intermediate program that translates English language instructions into the language of the computer), and coined the term "bug" to describe a computer glitch after her team found a moth in the machinery. Her work provided the foundation for digital computing. (www.cs.yale.edu/homes/tap/Files/hopper-story.html)

6. Nannerl
Musician, composer and older sister of Wolfgang Amadeus Mozart, Maria Anna "Nannerl" learned to play the harpsichord at age seven, and toured Europe with her brother to showcase their talents—sometimes receiving top billing. At age 18, however, her father stopped her from performing as she had reached marriageable age, and it was not appropriate for women to have a career. She was forced to stay at home where she taught music. (http://en.wikipedia.org/wiki/Maria_Anna_Mozart)

The Family Tree

A person's ancestral lineage is an exponential function. Assuming no shared ancestors, if we count back 40 generations (about 1,000 years), each person alive would have about a million billion ancestors.

The formula is 2^n

(2 = # of parents; n = # of generations)

Individual today: $2^0 = 1$
Parents: $2^1 = 2$
Grandparents: $2^2 = 4$
Great-grandparents: $2^3 = 8$
10th generation: $2^{10} = 1,024$
40th generation: $2^{40} = 1,100$ billion
= 1.1 trillion

A Letter from Bella

This note was received from the 12-year-old daughter of one of our recent training participants. Bella asked that her letter be shared with the entire group.

Hello, My name is Bella and I am writing this letter to thank you for what you are doing. I have gone through prejudice at ~~school~~ school and it has gotten so bad I did not want too go to school any more.

I am truly thankful what your doing and I really appreciate.

From: Bella

(Excuse the Spelling and mess + handwriting)

Teacher Expectations & Student Achievement

1. "A Different Kind of Classroom," by Robert Marzano,
   Association for Supervision & Curriculum Development, 1992.

2. "Classroom Interactions & Achievement," Mid-Continent Regional Educational Lab,
   quoted in ESD 105 "Class" newsletter, Oct. 1997.

3. "Closing the Achievement Gap Requires Multiple Solutions,"
   Northwest Educational Lab, May 1997.

4. "Do Teacher Expectations Matter?" by Nicholas Papageorge and Seth Gershenson, Sept. 2016.
   < www.brookings.edu/blog/brown-center-chalkboard/2016/09/16/do-teacher-expectations-matter >

5. "Examine Your Expectations: Teachers & Cultural Styles," Center for National Origin,
   Race & Sex Equity of the Northwest Regional Educational Laboratory, Oct. 1997.

6. "Expectations & 'At-Risk' Children," Rethinking Our Classrooms:
   Teaching for Equity & Justice, 1994.

7. "Guidelines for Effective Teaching," by Joyce Kaser, Mid-Atlantic Center for Race Equity.
   < www.amzn.com/B00072RD7Y >

8. "Kids Know What Teachers Expect," Harvard Education Letter, July/Aug 1992.

9. "Looking in Classrooms," by Thomas Good and Alyson Lavigne,
   Routledge Publishing, 11th edition, 2018. < www.amzn.com/1138646539 >

10. "Pygmalion Grows Up: A Model for Teacher Expectation Communication and Performance
    Influence," by Harris M. Cooper, Sage Journals, Review of Educational Research, Sept. 1979.

11. "Pygmalion in the Classroom: Teacher Expectation and Pupils' Intellectual Development,"
    by Robert Rosenthal, Crown House Publishing, May 4, 2003, ISBN-13: 978-1904424062.

12. "Race Biases Teachers' Expectations for Students: White teachers more likely to doubt
    educational prospects of black boys and girls," Johns Hopkins University.
    < http://releases.jhu.edu/2016/03/30/race-biases-teachers-expectations-for-students >

13. "Relationships Among Achievement, Low Income & Ethnicity," by Abbott & Joireman,
    WA School Research Center, Seattle Pacific University, Oct. 2001. < www.spu.edu/orgs/research >

14. "Summary of Research on Teacher Expectations & Student Achievement," by Michaelle
    Kitchen & Johnetta Hudson, Midwestern State University, 1998.

15. "Teacher Expectations Matter," by Nicholas Papageorge, Seth Gershenson & Kyungmin Kang,
    IZA DP No. 10165, August 2016. < http://ftp.iza.org/dp10165.pdf >

16. "The Effects of Teacher Beliefs on Teaching Practices and Achievement of Students With Disabilities," by Mary Klehm, Teacher Education and Special Education: Journal of the Teacher Education Division of the Council for Exceptional Children, March 2014. < http://journals.sagepub.com/doi/abs/10.1177/0888406414525050 >

17. "The Impact of Teacher Expectations on Student Achievement," by Lisa Kohut, Doctoral dissertation, Indiana University of Pennsylvania, 2014. < https://eric.ed.gov/?id=ED568494, ERIC Number: ED568494 >

18. "Two Decades of Research on Teacher Expectations: Findings and Future Directions," by Thomas L. Good, Sage Journal of Teacher Education, July 1987. < http://journals.sagepub.com/doi/abs/10.1177/002248718703800406 >

Excerpt from "Looking in Classrooms," by Good and Lavigne
"Teaching has more influence on student learning than any other variable that can be used to improve student potential...Obviously teachers cannot eliminate all the factors that impede student growth, including unequal funding of schools, poverty, nutrition and violence. However, teachers can influence student performance in important ways.

"...teachers form and communicate expectations to students and...those expectations in some cases reduce or improve student opportunities to learn through the provision of more support and more demand for performance from students who are believed to be more capable. Or alternatively, less performance because of less support and less demanding academic opportunities.

"Teachers hold judgments about the ability level of their students, and their beliefs about student ability can influence how they interpret students' actions (for one student, looking at the floor after being asked a question by the teacher might be seen as embarrassment, but the same behavior from a student believed to be more capable might be seen as thinking). These different teacher inferences lead to different consequences for students. In one case, the student is given up on by the teacher; in the other case, the teacher continues to demand student attention and response."

* * * * *

From "Do Teacher Expectations Matter?" by Papageorge and Gershenson
"Moreover, we find that teacher expectations differ by racial groups in a way that puts black students at a disadvantage, exacerbating racial achievement gaps."

* * * * *

From "Race Biases Teachers' Expectations for Students," Johns Hopkins Univ.
"What we find is that white teachers and black teachers systematically disagree about the exact same student. One of them has to be wrong."

UNITYWORKS
Diversity Training Institute

How is your district addressing cultural competence as a key strategy for closing the educational opportunity gap? Do teachers have the knowledge, skills and attitudes needed to effectively serve all students? Do all staff understand the impact of unconscious bias and institutional racism? What steps are being taken to improve equity and inclusion?

The UnityWorks Summer Institute is an action-packed, week-long annual professional learning event designed to prepare educators with the knowledge, tools, strategies and resources needed to address these questions, and to design and carry out a successful Diversity Action Plan. Sessions will be held Mon-Fri, from 8:30-4:30. Thirty-five clock hours available.

LEARN MORE

www.unityworks.org > School Program

info@unityworks.org, 877-899-1913

Space is limited (maximum 40).
Register early to guarantee your spot.

What People Are Saying

"Best professional development I ever attended! I want more!"

"An amazing week. Time well spent!"

"The training has been an eye-opener, for me and my staff."

"I left feeling empowered, energized and hopeful!!!"

"All teachers and administrators should take this course."

What Is Included?

Fee includes lunch, refreshments, workbook and all course materials. See our website for current rates, with discounts for teams and administrators.

Reflections

INDEX

Made in the USA
Columbia, SC
15 June 2019